THE RISE & FALL OF MUSLIM CIVIL SOCIETY

Omar Imady, PhD

For information, contact
MSI Press
784 Northridge PMB 293
Salinas, CA 93906
editor@msipress.com

Library of Congress Control Number 2005927102

ISBN 1-933455-03-9

Cover by Carl D. Leaver; cover photo by Yasir Sakr

Printed in the United States of America

To Mahmoud El-Kati & George Makdisi
I am still in your classrooms...

Contents

Omar Imady

Notes

- The transliteration system applied in this work is a simplified form of that of the Library of Congress. Arabic proper names, however, that are commonly found in English literature appear in their familiar Latinized form.
- All translations contained in this book are by the author unless otherwise indicated.

Omar Imady

Acknowledgments

This work is primarily indebted to my advisor and members of my doctoral committee: Dr. Thomas Naff, Dr. Roger Allen, Dr. Arthur Goldshmidt, and Dr. Frederick Frey. Indeed, their valuable insights permeate the entire text.

Without the support and encouragement of Dr. Betty Lou Leaver, this work would still be on the shelves designated for PhD dissertations in the Van Pelt Library at the University of Pennsylvania.

I would also like to thank Ms. Anna Jacobson for the wonderful job she did on copyediting the text and Mr. Carl Leaver for his meticulous work on preparing the book for printing.

Finally, I would like to express my deep appreciation to my two intellectual companions: Dr. Yasir Sakr and Dr. Khalid Blankenship.

Omar Imady

Preface

This work constitutes a revised and updated version of a PhD dissertation submitted to the Department of Asian and Middle Eastern Studies, School of Arts and Sciences, at the University of Pennsylvania (December 1993). It documents the account of four major Muslim reformers who, through their charismatic personalities and creative energy, succeeded in unleashing a process that eventually transformed the institutional fabric of Muslim countries. The account sheds light on a number of dramatic shifts, i.e. from orality to print culture, from that which is expressive to that which is instrumental, and from that which is tangible and personalized to that which is abstract and depersonalized. However, it is also the account of how a beautiful idea, i.e. Islamic reform, was transformed, as a direct, yet unintended, result of the process of institutional change initiated by these Muslim reformers, into what came to be known as Islamic fundamentalism.

There were two major reasons why I chose to focus on the factors underlining the rise of Islamic fundamentalism. First, I strongly felt, and despite the wealth of works produced on this subject over the last twelve years, still continue to feel, that many current attempts to understand the rise of Islamic fundamentalism on the basis of religious and/or contextual grounds are inherently inadequate.

Islam has been portrayed by the West (curiously forgetting the centuries prior to its own Enlightenment, when religion or its abuse was a primary force in politics and a catalyst to wars) as though it contains, as part of its historical legacy, a predilection to use religious ideas to vindicate the rise and fall of states and the use of violence against others. Thus, I could not subscribe to arguments that sought to explain Islamic fundamentalism as a function of the very nature of Islam. Likewise, I could not subscribe to arguments that sought to present a contextual explanation to the rise of Islamic fundamentalism. I simply was aware of too many examples within Islamic history when occupation and poverty did not give rise to militant organizations. My dissatisfaction with religious and contextual explanations led me, eventually, to what I describe as an *institutional* explanation; namely, one that regards the very evolution of institutions utilized by Muslims over the last one hundred years as primarily responsible for the phenomenon of militant Muslim organizations that are indifferent to any type of moral authority that attempts to inhibit their indiscriminate utilization of violence.

The second reason behind my decision to focus on the factors underlining the rise of Islamic fundamentalism is more personal. I once identified myself with the movement of Islamic reform, but became disillusioned not only because it eventually evolved into Islamic fundamentalism, but also because religious scholars who still identify themselves with the legacy of Islamic reform do not, in my perspective, adequately condemn the indiscriminate use of violence by Muslim fundamentalists. Indeed, violence is condemned when Muslims are involved. But what possible spiritual sense does it make to condemn such acts only when Muslim women and children are the victims? Nor is it morally justified, as the findings of this work confirm, for Muslim reformers to continue to foster the utilization of institutions that, by their very structural nature, lend themselves to support the use of political and indiscriminate violence.

This work, thus, is a critique of a movement that I once admired, a movement that aimed at unleashing a spiritual and intellectual revival of Islamic civilization, but was distracted from its initial objectives and ultimately distorted. If this work contributes, however minimally, to the rise of a new Islamic reform movement that is unequivocally, both intellectually and institutionally, against the use of indiscriminate violence, it would have, no doubt, far exceeded its objectives.

Omar Imady, PhD
Fall, 2005

Introduction

Various scholarly explanations have been set forth regarding why Islamic reform, a movement preoccupied with reviving Islamic civilization and resisting Western colonialism through the creation of a Muslim civil society, was superseded, in the mid-twentieth century, by Islamic fundamentalism, a movement preoccupied with creating an 'Islamic state' by violence if necessary.[1] Such explanations can be classified into two major categories: 'traditional legacy', and 'external dynamics'.

The 'traditional legacy' category includes works that explain Islamic fundamentalism as a product of the traditional legacy of Islam, which makes no separation between religion and state and which promotes political violence through the emphasis it places on *jihad* or morally ordained struggle/resistance.[2] Muslim religious scholars, however, strongly discouraged violent political descent. Regarding the confrontation of government authority, Ibn Taymiyyah (d. 1328) wrote: "What is well known regarding the position of *Sunni*[3] religious scholars is that they do not sanction rebellions against rulers", and "Sixty years under an oppressive ruler is better than one night of anarchy."[4]

It is also true that political violence frequents Islamic history. Moral legitimacy for such violence, however, was provided by religious scholars belonging to heretical Muslim sects known for their militant character (e.g. *al-Hashashin*, or the Assassins, etc.). Not only did *Sunni* religious scholars highly discourage violence against the government, but they also articulated a sophisticated and complex approach to the use of violence, within the framework of *jihad*, that barred targeting children, women, religious figures (regardless of the religion they belonged to) and all those who are not directly engaged in the war effort against Muslims.[5] Thus, to portray the phenomenon of Islamic fundamentalism as an expression of Islam's traditional legacy is to ignore centuries in which the use of political violence was categorically rejected by *Sunni* religious scholars.

Recognizing the lack of a strong precedent within the *Sunni* traditional legacy for political violence, studies in the category of 'external dynamics' have presented Islamic fundamentalism as a reaction against "the growth of the nation state and the peculiar problems of the twentieth century."[6] Factors such as the failure of secular and/or national regimes to bring about economic prosperity, Israel's major victories in 1948 and 1967, and Iran's 'Islamic revolution' are usually emphasized by such studies. Clearly severe economic conditions and military defeats do tend to create an environment conducive to the rise of politicized and often violent movements. There are numerous historical examples, however, of such conducive climates that did not give birth to similar movements (e.g. post WWII Germany and Japan). Further, while it is clear that Iran's revolution fueled the enthusiasm for Islamic fundamentalism, it is equally clear that fundamentalist institutions existed long before Iran's revolution was even contemplated by its leaders.

A more accurate explanation of the rise of Islamic fundamentalism can be arrived at by focusing on its institutional background, that is, the process through which Western institutions were adopted by Muslim reformers during the late nineteenth/early twentieth century. The adoption of the journal, the association, the political party, and the paramilitary force by Muslim reformers, as documented by subsequent chapters, reflected a frame of mind that regarded institutions as non ideological objects which could be utilized by various types of movements, irrespective of their principles and the setting within which they were operating. It was only when the adopted institutions began to take on a life of their own that Muslim reformers realized that certain institutions, (the political party and the paramilitary force in particular) could not be appropriated to their agenda. While the political party shifted the focus of the reform movement from the community to the state, the paramilitary force shifted its focus from colonial resistance to political violence. By then, however, it was too late. What had been adopted from the West could no longer be returned.

Ironically, Islam had a similar institutional impact on the West during the Middle Ages. In *The Rise of Colleges*, George Makdisi argues that the scholarly system of the West has its roots in Islamic soil.[7] Europe's adoption of the Muslim *ijazat al-tadris* (the license to teach) during the Middle Ages irreversibly undermined its hierarchal system of learning which was previously monopolized by the Church. A horizontal scholarly system emerged which endowed the European scholar not only with the license to teach, but also with *ijazat al-ifta'*, or the license to profess an authoritative opinion, an act which was previously the exclusive right of 'the college of bishops in union with the pope'. Likewise, the use of the political party and the paramilitary force by Muslim reformers irreversibly altered the way in which they understood their relationship to the government and to the reform movement. In both cases, techniques belonging to other cultures were treated as neutral and in both cases they undermined traditional perceptions and attitudes, and proved potentially explosive.[8]

This study aims at documenting the link between the rise of Islamic fundamentalism and a process of institutional change which was carried out by four Muslim reformers: Jamal al-Din al-Afghani (d. 1897), Muhammad Abduh (d. 1905), Rashid Rida (d. 1935), and Hasan al-Banna (d. 1949). The process, which involved the relinquishing of the institutions of traditional Muslim community, i.e. *madrasah* (religious college), *tariqah* (spiritual order), and *ta'ifah* (artisan/merchant guild), aimed at creating a Muslim civil society that could both revive Islamic civilization and resist Western colonialism. The dichotomy between Western institutional form and the moral vision of Islamic reform, together with a consistently hostile government, are shown to have been the principal factors behind the rise of Islamic fundamentalism.

The historical context for this study is found in 'Part I' where (a) an overview of the forerunner for Muslim civil society, i.e. the traditional Muslim community, is presented; and (b) the introduction of the institutions of civil society by Jamal al-Din al-Afghani to the religious scholars of Egypt is documented. 'Part II' covers the major institutions of Muslim civil society, i.e. the utilization of the journal by Muslim reformers, the utilization of the association, the utilization of the political party, and, finally, the utilization of the paramilitary force. 'Part III' covers the fall of Muslim civil society by analyzing the primary factors underlying the rise of Islamic fundamentalism.

Omar Imady

Part I

The Rise of Muslim Civil Society

Omar Imady

Chapter 1

Muslim Traditional Community: The Forerunner for Muslim Civil Society

The Severe Trial

During the ninth century, the Abbasid *khalifah*[1] al-Mamun (r. 813-833) set out to convert *ahl al-sunnah*, or the traditionalists who emphasized the authority of the Qur'an and Prophetic traditions, to a theological doctrine held by the *Muʿtazilah*, or the rationalists who emphasized the authority of reason and philosophical principles.[2] Traditionalist scholars were forced to recant their belief in the non-created nature of the Qur'an in favor of the rationalist doctrine which held that the Qur'an was a creation of God. Those who refused were tortured and, at times, executed. In 848, fifteen years after the beginning of the government sponsored inquisition, termed *al-Mihnah*, or the Severe Trial, by Muslim historians, al-Mutawakkil (r. 847-861) ordered the end of all government sponsored attempts to enforce the rationalist doctrine. Al-Mutawakkil's decision reflected his awareness that the inquisition had simply not succeeded and that its continuation might well inspire a popular revolt.

Prior to the Severe Trial, religious learning among the traditionalists was largely informal. In order to ensure that such a crisis would not reoccur, the traditionalists: "formed themselves into guilds, created institutions of learning and clothed themselves with the protective mantle of legal perpetuity."[3] At the core of the *madhahib* (guilds of law) created by the traditionalists was the *madrasah* (religious college).[4] While traditionalist scholars constituted the administrative force of the religious college, *waqf* (charitable religious trust) constituted its financial base.[5] In institutionalizing their victory, traditionalist scholars ensured that the laws they derived from the Qur'an and Prophetic tra-

7

ditions, including those regulating the religious college, would not be altered by government authority. Furthermore, in presiding over the administration of the religious college, traditionalist scholars ensured that heterodoxy, i.e. rationalism, would infiltrate neither its curriculum nor its faculty, at least not directly. Finally, in basing the religious college on the charitable religious trust, traditionalists ensured that it would remain private, and thus autonomous, from the state. Inspired by traditionalist scholars, *shuyukh al-turuq al-sufiyyah* (Masters of the spiritual orders) created a parallel system, known as the *tariqah* (spiritual order).[6] As was the case with the religious college, the charitable religious trust financed the *zawaya* (spiritual retreats/centers) of the spiritual orders, thereby further ensuring their autonomy from the state. Contrary to their popular image, the vast majority of spiritual centers were not in conflict with traditionalism. As stipulated by the regulations of the charitable religious trust, many spiritual centers taught law, the traditionalist science *par excellence.*[7]

With the emergence of the guilds of law and spiritual orders and the merger of the latter with the *futuwwah* (chivalrous brotherhoods) and the *tawa'if* (the guilds of merchants and artisans), the emergence of the institutions of traditional Muslim community was completed. On the eve of the Mongols' devastating invasion of the central lands of Islam in the thirteenth century, these institutions had matured to such an extent that they would not only survive the catastrophe, but would also serve: "as the pattern on which the damaged tissues of Islamic life were slowly reconstructed."[8]

In the thirteenth century, however, the political appointment of a *mufti* (Muslim jurist) in Damascus became an important development in the relationship between the government and the *ʿulama'*, or religious scholars.[9] The subsequent regulations introduced by the Ottomans, particularly the creation of a hierarchy of jurists led by *Shaikh al-Islam* (The Grand Mufti) of Istanbul, significantly facilitated government control over religious scholars.[10] The Ottoman regulations created a system within which the strength of a *fatwa* (religious legal verdict) was a function not of its own merits or popularity, but, rather, of the status of its articulator in the hierarchy of jurists. Indeed, a religious legal verdict from the Grand Mufti provided the Ottoman Sultan with all the religious legitimacy he needed to implement a certain act, e.g. a declaration of war, legal reform, etc..[11]

The Muslim Traditional Community: The Model of Cairo

Egypt's significant autonomy from Ottoman control, which allowed it to escape many of the Ottoman regulations which were imposed on traditional institutions, along with the interdependent relationship of the Mamluk rulers with the religious scholars, created a setting within which:

> ...direct intervention and control of the civil authorities
> was limited in the judicial service; in all other branches
> of learned activity and organization neither the authorities

at Istanbul nor the local officials, though preserving a direct or indirect right of confirmation, interfered with the traditional institutions or with their personnel and methods.[12]

Reflecting the nature of its traditional institutions, the urban organization of Cairo was structured in such a way as to allow each entity to fulfill its own functions within its distinct territory. The activities of religious scholars took place primarily in the premier religious college, i.e. *al-Azhar*. Activities of the members of the spiritual orders took place in spiritual centers located throughout Cairo. The activities of members of the guilds of merchants and artisans took place in *al-suq* (the market place).[13] The self-governing tradition of each of these institutions was deep rooted; so too was their separation from government authority.[14] That these institutions operated in distinct realms did not, however, reflect disunity among them. During times of crises, the institutions of the traditional Muslim community acted in a highly coordinated manner. Upon a request by the religious scholars, the Masters of the spiritual orders would mobilize the heads of the guilds of merchants and artisans who, in turn, would mobilize the rank and file members. To the inhabitants of Cairo, this network of institutions mediated their interests with the ruling authorities, protected them from coercion and helped to defend them against external threats. That the religious scholars controlled the activation of this network indicates that they were the *de facto* leaders of Cairo's Muslim community.

Prior to the rise of Muhammad Ali in 1805, religious scholars asserted their role as the protectors of the urban populace against the oppressive policies of the Ottoman and Mamluk administrative and military leaders. Aware of the mobilizing capacity of the religious scholars, embodied in the network of institutions, Egypt's rulers took seriously the intercession of the religious scholars on behalf of members of the community. In *ʿAjaʾib al-Athar, the* primary source on late Ottoman Egypt, Abd al-Rahman al-Jabarti highlights the type of situations within which this network was activated by religious scholars. In his account, for example, of how al-Sharqawi responded to the oppressive tax decrees of Muhammad Bey al-Alfi, one of the major Mamluk figures of late Ottoman Egypt, al-Jabarti wrote:

> The peasants told al-Sharqawi that al-Alfi's agents had come to their village and treated them unjustly, asking of them that which they cannot bear [i.e. high taxes]... Al-Sharqawi was angered and went to *al-Azhar*. He asked the other religious scholars to join him and they closed the gates of the mosque. Then, they ordered people to close the markets and shops. The next day, the religious scholars met at the house of al-Sadat. People surrounded the house...in such a way so as to be seen by

> Ibrahim Bey [Ibrahim and Murad Bey were the two most powerful Mamluk leaders at the time]. Ibrahim, who had been informed before hand of their meeting, sent Ayyoub Bey *al-daftirdar* [the principal financial officer of the government] to them. So Ayyoub Bey went to them and asked them about their demands. The religious scholars replied: 'We want justice and the termination of oppression and moral transgression and the application of religious law and the termination of the innovations and the new taxes which you have introduced.'[15]

Al-Jabarti wrote that the religious scholars meeting with Yusuf Bey was followed by a period of negotiations which ended "in that they [the Mamluk leaders] repented and returned to God's law and affirmed their commitment to fulfill the conditions of the religious scholars."[16] Al-Jabarti's account reveals the process undertaken by religious scholars when facing a local crisis: A joint meeting to agree on a plan of action, ordering the market and shops closed, and demanding that large numbers of people gather in a specific area. Since no less than sixty percent of Cairo's civilian male population belonged to one of the spiritual orders and guilds of merchants and artisans, the number of people mobilized was significant.[17]

Far more drastic measures were also available to the religious scholars as illustrated by eyewitness accounts of Cairo's two uprisings against the French occupation. Accounts of the way in which Cairo's first uprising began, synthesized and paraphrased below, are particularly instructive:

> On Sunday, October 21, 1798, less than three months after the French victory at the Battle of the Pyramids, Cairo's shops closed and its minarets proclaimed an all out *jihad*, or a morally ordained struggle/resistance, against the French forces. Large numbers of people headed towards *al-Azhar*. Some carried weapons once hidden from French authorities. A number of *Azhar* students delivered speeches to rally those who had not joined the crowd around *al-Azhar*. Women stood on the roofs of houses, motivating the crowds with their loud voices. The number of the people which finally gathered around *al-Azhar* was approximately 15,000.[18]

During Cairo's second uprising (March 20, 1800), al-Jabarti informs us that Cairo's artisans manufactured weapons and its merchants guaranteed food supplies.[19] Such were some of the methods available to the religious scholars for popular uprising when deemed necessary. The French occupation severely discredited both the Ottomans, for their failure to defeat the French army, and the Mamluks, for their failure to protect Egypt from the French forces, their flight to Upper Egypt, and their subsequent cooperation with the French commanding officers, especially during Cairo's second revolt.[20] In the struggle for political power which ensued after the French withdrawal, Cairo was subjected to revolt twice; in 1804 against the Mamluks (followed in 1811 by Muhammad Ali's final destruction of their power in Egypt) and in 1805, against the Ottoman governor, making him the last governor of Egypt to be sent from the Sublime Porte. In both revolts, Cairo's inhabitants were assisted by Muhammad Ali and his troops. Muhammad Ali, an ambitious Ottoman army officer from Macedonia, made a secret agreement with Cairo's religious scholars in which he pledged to rule in accordance with their will in return for their support for his bid for power.[21] The religious scholars lived up fully to their words. They declared by religious decree the termination of the Ottoman governor's authority and mobilized all the segments of the population which they controlled through the spiritual orders and the guilds of merchants and artisans to support Muhammad Ali's troops.[22]

The Dismantling of The Muslim Traditional Community

Ironically, the new direct involvement of religious scholars in selecting their political leaders, rather than formalizing their political power, marked the beginning of their subordination to the state. Three years after coming to power, Muhammad Ali began to issue decrees which began the process of altering the role of all traditional institutions, transforming them from instruments of community power into instruments of government control. As documented by Afaf Loutfi al-Sayyid Marsot, F. de Jong, and Gabriel Baer, the extension of government authority in Egypt over the guilds of law, the spiritual orders and the guilds of merchants and artisans by Muhammad Ali was swift and categorical.[23] Muhammad Ali first attacked the financial lifeline of traditional institutions. In 1812, a decree proclaimed the confiscation of all *waqf* lands (land designated for the purpose of financing a religious charitable trust), a total of 600,000 *feddans* (a *feddan* is equal to 1.039 acres).[24] This was done in spite of the precepts of traditionalist doctrine which held the religious charitable trust as "irrevocable and constituted in perpetuity."[25] In so doing, religious scholars and Masters of the spiritual orders, along with their institutions, were now financially dependent on the government.[26] Muhammad Ali then proceeded to strike at the spiritual orders directly. A decree in 1812 amounted to the creation of a new position, *Shaikh Mashaikh al-Turuq al-Sufiyyah* (Master of all Masters of Spiritual Orders) through which government control over the spiritual orders could be applied.[27] The decree clearly aimed at severing the link between the religious scholars and the common individual. Thus, the "authority of turuq-based power positions occupied by the *ᶜulama*'was undermined and their power consequently reduced."[28] Subsequent laws proclaimed or sanctioned by Muhammad Ali's successors, i.e. the Regulation of Spiritual Orders of 1895, their Amendments in 1903, and the Internal Regulations of 1905, further subordinated the spiritual orders to government control.[29] Nor were the guilds of merchants and artisans spared. Under the pressure of government actions and regulations, as well as European competition, the guilds declined, and by World War I disappeared.[30] It is, indeed, instructive to find that during the 1882 Urabi Revolt, the guilds (in contrast to their role in 1805) served as mechanisms of government control over the common members of the community. Indeed, it was through the guilds that the government communicated its instructions to the urban populace against public congregations and mistreatment of Europeans.[31]

The confiscation of the religious charitable trust and the regulation of spiritual orders and the guilds of merchants and artisans which took place during the nineteenth century left religious scholars without any effective institutional base; and, as a direct result, left members of the community under the direct authority of the state.

> Muhammad Ali...closed the one channel of opposition
> to tyranny that Egypt had known for centuries. The
> traditional bridge between ruler and ruled had gone, and
> there was nothing to replace it for many decades...[32]

In the 1870s, however, more than half a century after Muhammad Ali's decrees, Muslim reformers began to introduce Western institutions to Egypt's religious scholars. Rather than being content with their government salaries and internal rivalry, as Muhammad Ali and his successors had hoped, Egypt's religious scholars, and subsequently those of other Muslim countries, adopted these institutions and created, in the process, a Muslim civil society.

Chapter 2

Planting the seeds of Muslim Civil Society: (1871-1879)

The Activist: Jamal al-Din al-Afghani

Although Iranian and *Shiʿi*[33] by birth, Jamal al-Din al-Afghani (1838-1897) was known to most of his contemporaries as a *Sunni*[34] Afghan.[35] He described himself as such out of purely practical considerations, namely, to avoid being dismissed by religious scholars and political leaders of *Sunni* Muslim countries. In actuality, however, al-Afghani was neither a *Shiʿi* nor a *Sunni*. His world-view, rather, was a synthesis of *tasawwuf* (an approach to Islam that empha-sizes the spiritual experience, henceforth: sufism) and philosophy, combined with an intense inclination towards political activism. Al-Afghani was trained as a traditional scholar in Iraq and was, seemingly, self-taught in Western phi-losophy and political institutions during his subsequent stay in India. After liv-ing in Afghanistan (1866-1868), where he was involved in anti-British activity and in Istanbul (1869-1871), where his ideas aroused the hostility of religious scholars, al-Afghani moved to Egypt where he was destined to play a highly significant role in the rise of the national movement known as the Urabi Revolt. After being deported from Egypt in 1879, al-Afghani traveled to India and sub-sequently to Paris where in 1884 he founded *al-ʿUrwah al-Wuthqa* (The Firm Bond), the name given to both a political journal and a secret association. Al-Afghani subsequently turned his attention to Iran where he eventually played an important role in the Tobacco Uprising of 1891. His final years were spent in Istanbul, plotting against the Shah of Iran, propagating the Pan-Islamic project sponsored by the Ottoman Sultan and lecturing to a group of loyal students. In 1897, at the age of fifty nine, al-Afghani died, leaving behind a rich legacy of thought which remains a source of inspiration to Muslims of various tendencies and affiliations.

The Vision: Islamic Reform

Al-Afghani's approach to Islam, the *ummah* (Global Community of Muslims), and political authority, was destined to become the intellectual cornerstone of the movement known as *al-islah al-islami* (Islamic reform). It may be summarized as follows: Islam, in its 'purest form', is far removed from the rigid legalism and trivial disputations which religious scholars, *Sunni* and *Shiᶜi* alike, ascribe to it.[36] Islam, he maintained, is a religion of reason and progress. Further, Islam demands from its adherent's unity and collective action. Religious scholars must, therefore, shed their differences and reform their religious thought accordingly. Islam is also an egalitarian religion. *Shura*, or the principle of mutual consultation among *ahl al-hal wa-al-ᶜaqd*, or the representatives of Muslims, is the precept by which Islam declares the political equality of all believers. On the institutional level, al-Afghani believed that Muslim rulers must reform their political structures and allow their subordinates to play a role in the decision making process. More importantly, and in order to regain their once prominent role as leaders and defenders of the Muslim community, religious scholars, he felt, must relinquish the institutions of traditional Muslim community which have become instruments of Government control. The time had come for the emergence of a Muslim civil society, sanctioned by the state and protected by the law, where religious scholars, along with others, articulated their views through journals and mobilized the masses through associations and political parties.

Unlike the traditional Muslim community where traditional institutions had primarily a religious nature and were, thus, confined to Muslims, civil institutions have primarily a civic nature and are, thus, open to all citizens, Muslims and non-Muslims alike. Furthermore, while traditional institutions derived their legitimacy from religious precepts, civil institutions derive their legitimacy from a legal framework that, at least theoretically, cannot be superseded or tampered with by the state. To what extent al-Afghani was aware of how the concept of civil society had evolved from the works of Adam Ferguson (1723-1816), to Thomas Paine (1737-1809), to Hegel (1770-1831), and, finally, to de Tocqueville (1805-1859) is not clear. What is clear, however, is that al-Afghani was active at a time (the late nineteenth century) when the concept of a civil society, along with its institutions, in the West had matured to the extent of recognizing the need to protect and consistently renew a pluralistic, self-organizing civil society independent of the state.[37]

The Setting: Late 19ᵗʰ Century Egypt

During his stay in Egypt (1871-1879), al-Afghani's construction of an intricate network of journals and associations, despite its failure to achieve its designated objectives, succeeded in introducing Western institutions to Egypt's religious scholars at a time when traditional parallel institutions had lost much of their capacity to organize and rally the populace. Indeed, three types of institutions existed in late nineteenth century Egypt: the official, the traditional and the imported. The official type included *al-Waqa'i° al-Misriyyah* (The Official Gazette), founded in 1828, and *Majlis al-Nuwwab* (Assembly of Delegates or Parliament), founded in 1866; both of which were under the strong control of Khedive Ismail.[38] While *al-Waqa'i° al-Misriyyah* was used to announce government decrees, the Assembly of Delegates was used to facilitate the collection of taxes. The traditional type included: religious colleges, spiritual centers and guilds of merchants and artisans; all of which had come, as noted above, under significant government control daring the early nineteenth century. The imported type was represented by secret associations, including Freemasonry, and political journals, which, until the early 1870's, were directed towards the European immigrant population and had only a symbolic relationship with the local setting.[39]

Al-Afghani's Egyptian experience coincided with significant political instability not only in Egypt, but also in the Ottoman Empire as a whole. The declaration of bankruptcy of 1875, and the loss of territory brought about by the Serbo-Turkish war of 1876 and the Russo-Turkish war of 1877-1878, significantly weakened the empire's status. In Egypt, the recent past had witnessed the French occupation and the subsequent military and industrial failures which took place during Muhammad Ali's reign.[40] Ismail (1863-1879), Muhammad Ali's fifth successor, had not only imposed heavy taxes to finance such major projects as the Suez Canal and Cairo's Opera House, but had also opened the door to European intervention in Egypt's affairs. His severe mismanagement of the country's finances resulted in national bankruptcy, the Commission of Inquiry of 1878 and Dual Control (i.e. of the Egyptian economy by the government and European creditors).[41] Further destabilizing the conditions in Egypt were poor harvests caused by unusually low Nile floods, resentment towards European and Levantine traders who controlled the buying and selling of Egypt's major crops, and the failure of Egyptian industry to compete with European products.

The Cadre & the Plan

Almost immediately after his arrival in Cairo, al-Afghani began to propagate his vision of reform. Forced to stop preaching at *al-Azhar*, after its faculty accused him of preaching heretical views, al-Afghani resorted to lecturing in his home to a small number of students.[42] When his home was attacked by *Azhar* instigated mobs, he moved his *halaqah*, or study group, to Cairo's coffee shops, a setting viewed with contempt by religious scholars in nineteenth century Egypt.[43] Surrounded by his students, al-Afghani lectured on various topics including philosophy and astronomy, both of which had been excluded from the curriculum of the religious college since the traditionalists' victory over the rationalists in the ninth century.[44] His discourse captivated his listeners by virtue of its mystic orientation and its frequent references to Western philosophers and discoveries.[45]

Al-Afghani worked out a plan of action which aimed at resisting Western intervention in Egypt and the advancement of constitutional rule. The plan consisted of three major stages: recruitment, preparation, and implementation. First, al-Afghani selected and recruited to his cause a small number of individuals from among those who attended his lectures (see Table 1). These individuals were marked by their eagerness to become devout disciples of al-Afghani. Second, al-Afghani trained the selected individuals in journalism and political activism. Third, after approximately four years of such training, al-Afghani began to direct his students towards the actual application of their lessons.[46] The organized activity of al-Afghani and his students included (i) the establishment of five journals and newspapers: *Abu Nazzarah Zarqa'* (The Man With The Blue Glasses), *Jaridat Misr* (Egypt), *al-Tijarah* (Commerce), *Mir'at al-Sharq* (The Mirror of the Orient), and *Misr al-Fatat* (Young Egypt—the journal of the association of the same name); (ii) joining secret associations, i.e. *Mahfal Kawkab al-Sharq* (Lodge of the Orient Star); and (iii) the creation of associations, e.g. *al-Jamᶜiyyah al-Khayriyyah al-Islamiyyah* (The Islamic Benevolent Association) and *Misr al-Fatat* (Young Egypt).

Articulating the Vision: Journals

During the French occupation (1798-1801), French officers printed a number of proclamations in Arabic to the local inhabitants and founded a French newsletter, directed mainly towards the French soldiers.[50] Twenty seven years after the withdrawal of the French forces, Muhammad Ali founded *al-Waqa'iᶜ al-Misriyyah* (The Official Gazette). *Al-Waqa'iᶜ al-Misriyyah*, which was printed in both Arabic and Turkish twice a week and remained a unique publication until 1866, when the biweekly *Wadi al-Nil* (The Nile Valley) was founded in Cairo by Abd Allah al-Suᶜud.[51] *Wadi al-Nil*, however, was subsidized by Khedive Ismail and, thus, supportive of his policies.[52] In 1869, Ibrahim al-Muwaylihi and Uthman Jalal founded the weekly *Nuzhat al-Akhbar* (Stroll Through the News) which, unlike its predecessor, was somewhat critical of government policies. Two weeks after its appearance, it was banned.[53]

A more favorable climate for political journalism did not appear until the mid 1870's when Khedive Ismail, desiring to project a positive image to blunt the increasing criticisms and demands of England and France, allowed the founding of a number of journals which often contained criticism of his policies. With the notable exception of the weekly *al-Ahram* (The Pyramids), established by the Taqla brothers, almost every political journal founded in this new climate was indebted to the inspiration, literary training, and, at times, the legal and financial assistance of al-Afghani. As noted above, al-Afghani trained

Table 1: Al-Afghani's Students

NAME	NATIONALITY	RELIGION	EDUCATION
*Abd Allah al-Nadim	Egyptian	Muslim	Traditional
*Muhammad Abduh	Egyptian	Muslim	Traditional
*Ibrahim al-Laqqani	Egyptian	Muslim	Traditional
*Abd al-Salam al-Muwaylihi	Egyptian	Muslim	Traditional
*Ibrahim al-Muwaylihi	Egyptian	Muslim	Traditional
Sa'd Zaghlul	Egyptian	Muslim	Traditional
Abd al-Karim Salman	Egyptian	Muslim	Traditional
Ahmad Abu Khatwa	Egyptian	Muslim	Traditional
Shaikh Daghir	Egyptian	Muslim	Traditional
Ibrahim al-Hilbawi	Egyptian	Muslim	Traditional
Muhammad Bakhit	Egyptian	Muslim	Traditional
Abd al-Rahman Qara'ah	Egyptian	Muslim	Traditional
Abu al-Wafa al-Quni[47]	Egyptian	Muslim	Traditional
Yaqub Sannu[48]	Egyptian	Jewish	Modern
Adib Ishaq	Syrian	Christian	Modern
Salim al-Naqqash	Syrian	Christian	Modern
Salim al-Anhuri[49]	Syrian	Christian	Modern

(*) Students of al-Afghani who were chosen by him to be trained in journalism and political activism.

his students in political journalism as part of his overall plan to resist Western intervention and propagate constitutional rule. Although we do not have actual transcripts of al-Afghani's lectures on political journalism, a number of primary accounts have emphasized al-Afghani's role in teaching his disciples how to write journalistic essays, a genre of writing with which many of his traditionally educated disciples were unfamiliar.[54] Other accounts have also emphasized his role in acquiring licenses for a number of journals and even financial assistance to purchase the necessary equipment for the establishment of a printing press.

The rise of political journals, inspired and assisted by al-Afghani, coincided with the Turko-Russian War (1877-1878). Al-Afghani and his disciples, as Muhammad Abduh would later write, took advantage of people's desire to keep up with the War's progress, publishing journals which moved quickly from the mere reporting of the war's events to criticism of Khedive Ismail, Western intervention, and the advocacy of constitutional reform.[55] In March 1877, a satiric political newspaper in colloquial Arabic appeared in Cairo. This was *Abu Nazzarah Zarqa'*, the first political journal inspired by al-Afghani to appear in Egypt. Its founder was Yaqub Sannu, the talented Jewish Egyptian nationalist.[56] After fifteen issues full of unprecedented criticism of government policies, Khedive Ismail ordered it closed down. Sannu, however, traveled to France where, in 1878, he resumed the publication of *Abu Nazzarah Zarqa'* and copies found their way back into Egypt. The following excerpt illustrates its style:

> Abu Nazzarah proclaimed to you in the past: 'Your end will be as dark as tar...because you are the most oppressive of all oppressors in our age. Put an end, oh Ismail, to your transgressions so that old and young people may like you'. But you did not listen, oh Ismail, to my words...[57]

Two months after *Abu Nazzarah Zarqa'* was banned, another Afghani-inspired newspaper surfaced. Founded by Adib Ishaq in Cairo, *Misr* quickly became not only the major mouthpiece of al-Afghani's views, but also one of the major Egyptian newspapers of its day.[58] Having been helped by al-Afghani in acquiring a permit, and in purchasing necessary equipment, Ishaq proceeded to spread the views of his teacher. Subsequently, al-Afghani asked Ishaq to transfer the location of *Misr* to Alexandria to facilitate the attainment of foreign news. An article which was published in *Misr* in May 24, 1879, illustrates the extent to which this newspaper was a mouthpiece of al-Afghani. The occasion of the article was a lecture given by al-Afghani in Alexandria in the *Zizinyah* auditorium. Ishaq writes:

> ...the *Zizinyah* auditorium was full of intelligent people who, from their chairs and balconies, stared at the wise and noble soul residing in the body of our master and teacher. The ears opened, as it were, to capture the jewels of his wise words...[59]

Al-Afghani also helped Salim al-Naqqash, whom he had asked to join Adib Ishaq in Alexandria, to get a permit for *al-Tijarah*.[60] *Al-Tijarah* made an agreement with *Reuters*, the world news agency, and thereby became the first Egyptian newspaper to have such a connection. After a two week suspension in 1879 for attacking the European cabinet of Nubar Pasha—Egypt's Prime Minister (August, 1878-Feburary, 1879)—*al-Tijarah* continued its highly critical tone and was shut down, along with *Misr*, in November 1879. It is worth noting that the nationalist tone of both *Misr* and *al-Tijarah* gradually intensified over the years, reaching their peak shortly before their termination. This is most apparent in the case of *al-Tijarah* since it began as an exclusively financial newspaper. In February 1879, al-Afghani helped Salim al-Anhuri acquire a permit for *Mir'at al-Sharq*. Subsequently, al-Anhuri published *Mir'at al-Sharq* from his own printing press, *al-Iitthad* (The Union).[61] In April 1879, al-Anhuri, fearful of Egypt's explosive climate, decided to return to Lebanon. Thus, Ibrahim al-Laqqani, second only to Abduh in proximity to al-Afghani, took over the publication of *Mir'at al-Sharq. Mir'at al-Sharq was* shut down when al-Laqqani objected to al-Afghani's deportation, late in August 1879.

In addition to his involvement with *Misr* and *al-Tijarah,* Adib Ishaq was also involved in editing *Misr al-Fatat* which was printed in Arabic and French.[62] *Misr al-Fatat* appeared in Alexandria in 1879, shortly before the end of the reign of Ismail. Claiming to represent Egypt's youth, it proceeded to criticize the policies of Khedive Ismail. Shortly after Khedive Tawfiq took over, *Misr al-Fatat* published a proposal for constitutional reform. Tawfiq responded by ordering it shut down.[63] Though *al-Ahram*, as mentioned above, was not inspired by al-Afghani, it was, nevertheless, infiltrated by Abduh who succeeded in having a number of his essays published by its editorial board.[64] Al-Afghani is known to have also utilized a number of prestigious auditoriums, e.g. *Zizinyah* of Alexandria, to give lectures on various topics which were subsequently summarized and published by one of his loyal journals.[65] Apparently, an entry fee would be charged by the auditorium, thereby assuring an elitist audience.

Activating the Vision: Freemasonry

Accounts vary in regard to how and when Freemasonry arrived in Egypt. It seems very likely, however, that the first Masonic lodge, as Jurji Zaydan relates in *Tarikh al-Masuniyyah,* was founded in Cairo in 1798 by a number of French officers.[66] The lodge, named *Isis*, was founded for political purposes, namely, unifying local dignitaries into a single body to be manipulated by the French authorities.[67] Napoleon's withdrawal from Egypt did not fully terminate the activity of Freemasonry in Egypt, though it did cause its decline. Muhammad Ali's friendly attitude towards France seems to have allowed French Freemasons a significant degree of freedom which they utilized to their advantage, as their subsequent growth indicates.[68] French Freemasonry was soon to be followed by the more aggressive and politically motivated Italian Freemasonry which was brought to Egypt during the 1830's by a number of Italian Freemasons who had left Italy after the failure of their revolutionary activity.[69]

The 1840's witnessed important developments in the spread of Freemasonry in Egypt. In 1845, a French Chapter, *al-Ahram* (The Pyramids), was founded in Alexandria which embraced a number of important Muslim figures, such as Abd al-Qadir al-Jaza'iri, the well known Algerian resistance leader, and Prince Halim Pasha, the youngest son of Muhammad Ali.[70] In 1873 a number of Europeans belonging to different lodges succeeded in uniting European Freemasonry in Egypt under the umbrella of the *Grand Egyptian Orient*.[71]

Sensing the importance and potential danger of this unified institution, Khedive Ismail is reported to have granted an audience to S. F. Zola, its newly chosen Master. In return for granting his protection to the *Grand Egyptian Ori-*

ent, Khedive Ismail demanded that the new institution confine its activities to philanthropy.[72] Zola agreed, and by 1878, most chapters came under the jurisdiction of the *Grand Egyptian Orient*. The status of Freemasonry in Egypt during the 1870s in relation to other existent institutions was highly significant. To those Egyptians who were interested in advancing political objectives and who had no access to other institutions, Freemasonry was an ideal alternative.[73] Not only did Freemasonry provide secrecy—indispensable when dealing with an authoritative figure like Khedive Ismail—and a ready made institutional structure, but it also had the advantage of a special kind of security, embodied in the protection which European members could provide local members in times of need. Freemasonry was also reminiscent of the spiritual orders in that they both utilized initiation and symbolic language.[74]

Four years after his arrival in Egypt, al-Afghani began his organized activity against Khedive Ismail's policies and Western intervention by joining the Freemasons. His application reads as follows:

> I, Jamal al-Din al-Kabili [the one from Kabul] the philosophy teacher residing in Egypt who is thirty seven years old, request from *Ikhwan al-Safa'* [The Brethren of Purity] and call on the brothers of loyalty, by whom I mean the leaders of this holy Masonic lodge, which is far above falsehood and error, to be grateful toward me and endow their favors upon me by accepting me in this pure lodge and by allowing me to enter among those who have entered in this prestigious club.
>
> To you belongs gratitude.
>
> Thursday, 23, *Rabiᶜ al-Thani*, 1292 [May 29, 1875] Jamal al-Din al-Kabili.[75]

Al-Afghani's application provides three important insights. First, al-Afghani characterizes himself as 'al-Kabili' or the one from Kabul, rather than 'al-Afghani', the one from Afghanistan. As attested by this and other documents, name changing was a tactic which al-Afghani often used in his organized activity. Other known names used by al-Afghani, include 'al-Istanbuli', i.e. the one from Istanbul, and 'al-Husayni' or descendent of Husain, the grandson of the Prophet.[76]

Second, al-Afghani characterizes himself as a philosophy teacher. If others also referred to him as such, this would help explain at least some of *al-Azhar*'s hostility to al-Afghani, since among the subjects not admitted to the religious college, e.g. medicine, astronomy, etc., philosophy was the one viewed with the most contempt by *al-Azhar*'s religious scholars. Third, by making an analogy to *Ikhwan al-Safa'* in his application, al-Afghani shows himself to have perceived Freemasonry as an institution which had parallel with traditional Islamic associations. Like Freemasonry, *Ikhwan al-Safa'* was a secret organization which was responsible for producing a number of philosophical treatises.[77] Though its members are not known, they are suspected by scholars of having belonged to *al-Isma'iliyyah.*[78]

Unfortunately, al-Afghani's application does not specify the lodge he was applying to. Nevertheless, other documents indicate that al-Afghani first became involved with Italian lodges, a logical step given the highly politicized nature of Italian Freemasonry.[79] Though al-Afghani subsequently joined the more prestigious English and French Masonic lodges, his relationship with Italian Freemasonry, was maintained until his deportation from Egypt in 1879.[80]

Several documents make it clear that al-Afghani did join *Kawkab al-Sharq*, No. 1355, which was founded in Cairo in 1871 and which was affiliated with the *United Grand Lodge of England*. The first of these documents, dated January 24, 1877, contains an invitation to al-Afghani to attend a session at the lodge.[81] The second reveals the status which al-Afghani was able to reach within a period of two years. The document, dated January 7, 1878, invites al-Afghani to his confirmation as President of *Kawkab al-Sharq* for the year 1878.[82] Further documents show al-Afghani to have maintained his relationship with *Kawkab al-Sharq* until at least July 13, 1879.[83] Additional documents show that al-Afghani continued to reach out to Masonic lodges. He received an invitation, dated March 5, 1877, to attend a session at the *Grand Lodge of Egypt*, two invitations to *al-Nil*, affiliated to the *National Grand Lodge of Egypt*, dated May 2, 1878 and August 16, 1878 and an invitation to *Grecia*, affiliated to the *United Grand Lodge of England*, dated February 3, 1879.[84] Every thing else we know regarding al-Afghani's involvement with Freemasonry comes from the following sources, *Tarikh ʿAbduh, Khatirat al-Afghani,* and Muhammad Sabry's *La genese de l'esprit national egyptien (1863-1882)*[85] All sources agree, or at least do not object to, a number of points: Al-Afghani entered into Freemasonry, he led a lodge which included three hundred of Egypt's most important figures, including Crown Prince Tawfiq, Sharif Pasha, Butrus Pasha, Sulaiman Abaza Pasha—all three high ranking government officials—and he withdrew from at least one Masonic lodge. What the sources do not agree on is which lodge in particular embraced the three hundred members. While *La genese* associates the three hundred members with *Kawkab al-Sharq*, Muhammad al-Makhzumi in *Khatirat al-Afghani* and Adib Ishaq and Salim al-Anhuri in *Tarikh ʿAbduh* ascribe the three hundred members to a 'national' lodge.[86]

In attempting to solve this anomaly, Kudsi-Zadeh in his "Afghani and Freemasonry" asserts that al-Afghani first became involved in *Kawkab al-Sharq*.[87] On the basis of a passage in *La genese,* Kudsi-Zadeh relates the names of some of the figures who were members of *Kawkab al-Sharq* along with al-Afghani.[88] He does not, however, specify the number of persons who joined *Kawkab al-Sharq* under al-Afghani's patronage, though Sabry in *La genese* provides the number (three hundred). Kudsi-Zadeh then relates, on the basis of *Khatirat* and essays reproduced in *Tarikh ʿAbduh*, that al-Afghani withdrew from *Kawkab al-Sharq* and formed a 'national' lodge.[89] At this point, Kudsi Zadeh refrains from naming the important members who joined the 'national' lodge, though they are provided by *Khatirat* and *Tarikh ʿAbduh,* describing it only as having embraced three hundred members. In short, rather than address the fact that *La genese* describes *Kawkab al-Sharq* in the exact same manner *Khatirat* and *Tarikh ʿAbduh* describe the 'national' lodge, Kudsi-Zadeh suppresses certain components of *La genese* (the three hundred number) and certain components of *Khatirat* and *Tarikh ʿAbduh's* account (the names of some of the figures involved), that he may present his own reading of events, namely, that two separate lodges existed, as consistent with the information provided by the sources.

Even if one is to ignore Kudsi-Zadeh's treatment of the sources, his reading of events is still undermined by a very important problem. As indicated in documents specified above, al-Afghani remained part of *Kawkab al-Sharq* until at least July 13, 1879. We also know that al-Afghani was deported from Egypt in late August 1879. Thus, how could he have formed, over a one-month period, a 'national' lodge which boasted three hundred highly important figures? Since Kudsi-Zadeh's 'two lodges' theory cannot hold, one is tempted to dismiss either *Kawkab al-Sharq* or the 'national' lodge as fictitious. Yet, as previously stated, *Kawkab al-Sharq* is fully attested to by several documents. Further, the 'national' lodge is mentioned by a number of sources, the authors of which are known to have had no contact with each other, i.e. Adib Ishaq and Muhammad al-Makhzumi.

There is, however, another alternative, one that is in harmony with the sources and, equally important, with the elusive character of al-Afghani's political activity; specifically, that *Kawkab al-Sharq* and the 'national' lodge are one and the same. The former is what might be termed the 'outer' lodge which al-Afghani, along with his disciples, and many other important Egyptian figures joined. The latter is the 'inner' lodge, embracing only al-Afghani and his disciples which was created in response to the objection of members of *Kawkab al-Sharq* to al-Afghani's politicization of their structure. In so doing, al-Afghani enjoyed both the protection, derived from membership in a European lodge and the power, embodied in controlling the 'national' lodge. As such, one comes to understand why no name is ever provided by the sources, which refer to a 'national' lodge. Kudsi-Zadeh himself writes: "The name of the latter [i.e. the 'national' lodge] is yet to be determined."[90] More importantly, one comes to understand why the descriptions of the 'national' lodge and *Kawkab al-Sharq* are consistently identical. The 'inner lodge' appears to have also been a hidden structure underlying a number of other lodges as well, including *al-Nil*, noted above, which was affiliated with the *Grand French Orient*, the same affiliation Ishaq and al-Makhzumi ascribe to the 'national' lodge.[91] When members of the 'outer lodge' became suspicious about al-Afghani's plans, he and his disciples simply withdrew and affiliated themselves with another lodge, thereby giving rise to a number of accounts on al-Afghani's withdrawal from Freemasonry, including Rida's which dates al-Afghani's withdrawal as early as 1876.[92]

Activating the Vision: Associations

Closely associated with Freemasonry, yet distinct, was the phenomenon of associations.[93] The term *jamᶜiyyah* was perhaps first used to designate voluntary groupings by Christian missionaries in Syria who, during the late seventeenth/ early eighteenth century, formed *Jamᶜiyyat al-Mukhallis* (The Association of the Savior). Subsequently, the term began to be utilized in the mid-19th century to refer to various types of associations, including benevolent and learned, the latter usually having secret political aims hidden under an intellectual garb.[94] Such associations were unknown in Egypt prior to the French invasion.[95] *L'Institut d'Egypt*, founded by the French authorities in 1798 and terminated after their withdrawal, had to wait until 1859 to be reincarnated as an Egyptian 'national' entity, taking the name of *al-Maᶜhad al-ᶜIlmi al-Misri* (The Scientific Egyptian Institute). By 1870, several learned associations had been founded in Egypt, all reflecting a significant degree of Western involvement and sponsorship.

Al-Afghani did not become directly involved in open associations. Yet, by encouraging his disciples to create such institutions, his involvement was nonetheless important. *Misr al-Fatat*, founded in Alexandria in 1879, embraced a number of important disciples of al-Afghani, including Adib Ishaq, Salim al-Naqqash, and Abd Allah Nadim.[96] Its organ was a journal by the same name. When the association published a reform program shortly after Khedive Tawfiq's accession, it was banned, having lasted less than a year.[97] Abd Allah al-Nadim, apparently uncomfortable with the large number of non-Muslims in *Misr al-Fatat*, had left the association earlier and founded *al-Jamᶜiyyah al-Khayriyyah al-Islamiyyah* in 1878, which, as a number of authorities have indicated, seems to have been the first benevolent association in Egypt.[98] It was responsible for establishing a national school for boys and girls, and hosting various social activities, including plays and speech festivals.

Additional Institutions

Al-Azhar never relinquished its deep hostility toward al-Afghani. It was not successful, however, in fully preventing the advancement of al-Afghani's views within its own precincts. In spite of much opposition from some of his professors, Muhammad Abduh graduated from *al-Azhar* in 1876.[99] Subsequently, he began to teach at *al-Azhar* the much-disliked philosophy. Two years later, he was made a teacher of history at *Dar al-ᶜUlum* (Academy of Sciences) and of Arabic sciences (i.e. grammar and rhetoric) at *Madrasat al-Alsun al-Khidaywiyyah* (The Khedive School of Languages). Through another disciple, Abd al-Salam al-Muwaylihi, al-Afghani also utilized the Assembly of Delegates as a forum within which his views would be articulated and defended. Beginning in 1876, al-Muwaylihi became one of the most important defenders of the rights of the Assembly, sitting on almost all of its important committees.[100] Al-Afghani is also credited with encouraging Yaqub Sannu, who had earlier participated in founding the Egyptian theater, to utilize the medium of drama as a method for political mobilization. Thus, Sannu began to produce social and politically oriented plays, in response to which Ismail canceled a previously pledged stipend to his dramatic works.[101] The plays were performed in a theater located in old Cairo which was owned by Sannu. Although information on the actors who took part in these plays is scarce, we do know that Sannu himself at times performed.[102]

Al-Afghani's Institutional Network

The network of associations and journals inspired by al-Afghani was at the heart of the nationalist movement in the late nineteenth century. The nucleus of al-Afghani's network was the Masonic 'inner lodge', imbedded in at least two Masonic lodges—*Kawkab al-Sharq* and *al-Nil*—whose members were his closest disciples, including Abduh, al-Laqqani, al-Nadim, Ibrahim and Abd al-Salam al-Muwaylihi, Sannu, Ishaq and al-Naqqash. The 'outer lodge', on the other hand, served to acquaint al-Afghani and his disciples with Egypt's important personalities and served as a protective layer for their activity. Through the 'inner lodge', the four previously cited journals, *Abu Nazzarah Zarqa'*, *Misr*, *al-Tijarah and Mir'at al-Sharq* were published; and the two previously cited associations, *Misr al-Fatat* and *al-Jamᶜiyyah al-Khayriyyah al-Islamiyyah*, were created. While *al-Azhar*, *Dar al-ᶜUlum*, and *Madrasat al-Alsun al-Khidaywiyyah* were infiltrated by Abduh, the Assembly of Delegates was infiltrated by Abd al-Salam al-Muwaylihi. Further, a number of plays written by Sannu were performed.

This was not all. Members of the 'inner' lodge were also involved in contacting various government officials to help alleviate nationalist grievances. Thus, the Minister of Defense was urged to replace Egyptian officers who had been stationed for a long period in the Sudan with non-Egyptian officers as the law required, and the Minister of Justice, the Minister of Financial Affairs, and the Minister of Public Works and Royal Possessions were asked to treat their Egyptian employees fairly.[103] The various parts of the network were interwoven by the practice of cross-contributions by the 'inner' lodge's members. Al-Afghani, for example, contributed several articles to *Misr,* at times under a pseudonym, Mazhar Ibn Waddah.[104] Contributions to *Misr* and *Misr al-Fatat* were also made by Sannu, Naqqash, Nadim and Laqqani.

Al-Afghani's network rallied Egypt's elite towards the national cause through various Masonic lodges, propagated nationalist ideals among the urban populace, through various journals, and even showed how some of these ideals could be implemented by creating a school which emphasized love of country, through *al-Jamᶜiyyah al-Khayriyyah al-Islamiyyah*. Indeed, outside the realm of the army, all organized nationalist activity that was of any significance in

Egypt of the 1870s was initiated by al-Afghani and members of the 'inner lodge'.[105] That is not to say that only al-Afghani and his disciples held nationalist sentiments. *Azhar* religious scholars who were, as indicated above, very hostile toward al-Afghani were also strongly resentful of Western intervention. Nevertheless, al-Afghani and his disciples did dominate in the expression of all nationalist sentiments that were translated into institutional activity.

The most important project taken on by al-Afghani's network was its support of Ismail's abdication in favor of his son, Crown Prince Tawfiq. Al-Afghani had come to know Tawfiq through *Kawkab al-Sharq* and had succeeded in establishing a very close relationship with him. Tawfiq is reported to have repeatedly stated to al-Afghani: "My hopes for Egypt lie in you."[106] A number of events reveal the extent to which al-Afghani was supportive of Tawfiq. When, for example, al-Afghani heard that a number of Prince Abd al-Halim's supporters visited Tricou, the French Consul, and claimed that it was Abd al-Halim, rather than Tawfiq, who was supported by the majority of the people, al-Afghani quickly went to the French Counsel and emphasized the contrary. Al-Afghani is also credited with playing a prominent role in convincing Sharif Pasha to recommend to Ismail that he abdicate in favor of his son.[107]

Some studies have also suggested that al-Afghani even contemplated orchestrating an assassination of Khedive Ismail.[108] The evidence for this proposition, however, is derived exclusively from statements made by Wilfred S. Blunt, an author who in spite of the numerous insights he has provided by virtue of his personal relationships with both al-Afghani and Abduh, has been shown to have made inaccurate remarks about the activity of al-Afghani.[109] Al-Afghani has also been linked with the assassination of Shah Nasir al-Din, (1848-1896).[110] However, in both cases the evidence of al-Afghani's complicity is very slim and, most importantly, inconsistent with his writings, patterns of behavior, and what was said about him by his disciples who knew him best. Indeed, both Ismail and Nasir al-Din were regarded by al-Afghani as oppressive rulers who had facilitated Western intervention in their countries. None of his known lectures and writings, however, reflect a sanctioning of political violence. Nor did any of his closest disciples, e.g. Abduh, al-Nadim, Ibrahim and Abd al-Salam al-Muwaylihi—whose activity, one assumes, was reflective of their masters' ideals—ever became involved in political violence. Thus, the arguments against his advocacy of assassination as an instrument of policy heavily outweigh contrary claims.

In June 1879, Ismail abdicated and Tawfiq became the new ruler of Egypt. Less than three months later, Tawfiq ordered al-Afghani expelled from Egypt. According to al-Afghani, Khedive Tawfiq's decision to deport him was based on rumors that he sought the overthrow of the monarchy and the establishment of a republic.[111] Some of al-Afghani's disciples, on the other hand, have portrayed the French and British consuls as the figures responsible for convincing Tawfiq of the need to deport al-Afghani.[112] While such factors may have played a role in Tawfiq's decision, they would not have been sufficient if Tawfiq was a sincere follower of al-Afghani, as was Abduh for example. Tawfiq, rather, cynically used al-Afghani's network in his bid for power. He had no intention of living up to al-Afghani's ideals of national sovereignty and constitutional rule. As soon as he became the Khedive of Egypt, he moved against al-Afghani's network, just as his great grandfather, Muhammad Ali, had earlier done against the network of traditional institutions which played a significant role in his bid for power. After a harsh investigation by police, on August 30, 1879, al-Afghani was put on a boat to India.[113] With the exception of the refusal of *Mir'at al-Sharq* to publish a government-circulated article condoning al-Afghani's deportation, Tawfiq's decision was not protested.[114] Why did al-Afghani's network fail to protect him?

A number of explanations are found in the two major authorities on al-Afghani's activity in Egypt: Keddie's *al-Afghani* and Kudsi-Zadeh's "Afghani and Freemasonry." Both emphasize, to different degrees, the fact that Riyad Pasha, al-Afghani's chief protector, was in Europe at the time.[115] Further, al-Afghani is said to have lacked a strong relationship with the army. As for the two military officers which *La genese* describes as having been members of *Kawkab al-Sharq*, i.e. Latif Salim, and Said Nasr, Keddie dismisses their membership on account of not being mentioned by "earlier and more direct sources."[116] In short, al-Afghani's inability to defend against his deportation, according to Keddie and Kudsi-Zadeh, was a result of his reliance on influential individuals who, for various reasons, could not live up to his expectations, and his failure to establish a strong relationship with army officers.

Keddie's and Kudsi-Zadeh's explanations, however, are not convincing. On one hand, it does not seem likely that either Riyad Pasha nor Sharif Pasha could have stopped a determined Khedive Tawfiq from deporting al-Afghani, especially if he was supported in his decision by the European consuls, as seems to be the case, given their documented discomfort with al-Afghani's ideas and activity.[117] In addition, although Keddie's assertion, that sources earlier than Sabry (1924) do not confirm the presence of army officers in *Kawkab al-Sharq,* is contradicted by A. M. Broadly's *Arabi and His Friends* (1884), it appears highly improbable that supportive army officers at this early point could have used force to prevent al-Afghani's deportation.[118]

The more likely explanation is that al-Afghani's network was grounded foremost in a small educated elite, rather than the urban masses. It was al-Afghani's realization of the limitations of his network that appears to have prompted him to begin an intense campaign of public speeches after Tawfiq's betrayal of the nationalist cause became apparent. In a desperate move, al-Afghani hoped that the urban masses would respond to his call for a mass revolution.[119] The urban masses, however, as yet unaffected by al-Afghani's methods of mobilization, remained unmoved and Tawfiq, using al-Afghani's angry words as a pretext, moved against him. After al-Afghani was deported, his network received a number of blows which eventually resulted in its total collapse. Not only did authoritarian rule survive, but Egypt ultimately fell under total British control.

Nevertheless, al-Afghani's activity accomplished a profound, yet seemingly unintended, achievement. In creating his network, al-Afghani reintroduced to the Egyptian urban setting institutions which were significantly autonomous from government control. Having lost their traditional institutions to government authority, Egypt's religious scholars encountered in al-Afghani's network an alternative long awaited. Yet, the decision to join al-Afghani's network must have been exceptionally difficult. Not only was al-Afghani's network comprised of secular institutions, but also, joining al-Afghani's network was synonymous with acknowledging the impotence of *al-Azhar* when confronting the state. Why else would associations and journals be employed by al-Afghani, if not because of his perception that the capacity of *al-Azhar* to issue a religious legal verdict against government actions, and its capacity to mobilize the populace, if necessary, to enforce the verdict had become significantly eroded.

Though al-Afghani's unfamiliar discourse made it difficult for many religious scholars to follow him, it was the implications of his choice of Western institutions that was particularly discomforting. One suspects that many religious scholars simply did not want to acknowledge that *al-Azhar*, which had resisted Napoleon and appointed Muhammad Ali, was no longer capable of playing an important and independent role in the community. Thus, one understands why so many religious scholars opted to reject al-Afghani's invitation to reassert their role as leaders and defenders of their community in spite of their strong nationalist aspirations. Other religious scholars, however, found al-Afghani's invitation far too attractive to be resisted. Within al-Afghani's network, they actively pursued what they believed to be the proper future for their country. Indeed, not since the French occupation and Muhammad Ali's accession to power, did Egypt's urban centers witness religious scholars engaged in such intense political activity. That they did so peacefully along with non-Muslims, Christians and Jews, serves only to further highlight the magnitude of al-Afghani's achievement. Although al-Afghani's deportation from Egypt succeeded in causing the collapse of his network, it failed to erase from the memory of his followers their powerful experience. As will be seen, journals and associations sponsored by religious scholars gradually reappeared in Egypt. All were indebted to the institutional groundwork laid earlier by al-Afghani.

Part II

Institutions of Muslim Civil Society

Omar Imady

Chapter 3

Journals

Until at least the 1920s, newspapers and journals occupied the prestigious status of "the focal point of politics, in both Western and non-Western countries."[120] This was especially true in Egypt where by 1898, one hundred and sixty nine newspapers and journals had been established. By 1913, the number had increased to two hundred and eighty two.[121] In this 'era of journalism', Muslim reformers sponsored three major journalistic projects. The first involved Egypt's official newspaper, *al-Waqa'i° al-Misriyyah* (The Official Gazette), the second involved a political newspaper published in Paris, *al-°Urwah al-Wuthqa* (The Firm Bond), and the third involved a scholarly journal based in Cairo, *al-Manar* (The Beacon). Various factors forced both *al-Waqa'i° al-Misriyyah* and *al-°Urwah al-Wuthqa* to cease publication prior to achieving their objectives. *Al-Manar*, on the other hand, enjoyed a long life during which it succeeded in establishing a scholarly religious authority independent from that of the religious college.

Al-Waqa'i° al-Misriyyah (The Official Gazette)[122]

Muhammad Abduh met al-Afghani while still a student at *al-Azhar* and quickly became his most devout disciple.[123] Unlike Yaqub Sannu, Adib Ishaq, Salim al-Naqqash, and Ibrahim al-Laqqani, however, Abduh did not play a prominent role in the journalistic activities sponsored by al-Afghani. Abduh's primary activity, rather, was the propagation of al-Afghani's ideas through his teaching positions at *al-Azhar*, *Dar al-°Ulum* (The School of Sciences) and *Dar al-Alsun al-Khidaywiyyah* (The Khedive Language Academy). After al-Afghani was deported from Egypt in August 1879, Abduh was stripped of all of his teaching positions and was confined to his village, Mahallat Nasr.[124] Two months later, Riyad Pasha returned to Egypt, having been named the new Prime

Minister by Khedive Tawfiq. Riyad Pasha—one of the influential figures whom al-Afghani succeeded in befriending during his stay in Egypt—obtained a pardon for Abduh and, upon the recommendation of some of his advisors, Riyad appointed him third editor of *Waqa'i*.[125]

Riyad Pasha wanted *Waqa'i* transformed from a biweekly newsletter of new Government decrees and poems praising the Khedive into one of Egypt's popular daily newspapers.[126] In response to a request by Riyad Pasha, Abduh authored a reform program for *Waqa'i*, proposing several changes. Government agencies would be obliged to write reports to the editor-in-chief of *Waqa'i* informing him of their activities. Courts would also be obliged to write reports informing the editor-in-chief of their decisions. All reports of government agencies and courts were to be published in *Waqa'i*. The editor-in-chief would have the right to comment on the activities of official agencies. The editor-in-chief would also have the authority to supervise all newspapers published in Egypt, including those published in foreign languages; if a newspaper was found guilty of persistently publishing erroneous information, the editor-in-chief would have the right to suspend it temporarily or even permanently. Finally, essays written by the editors of *Waqa'i* would be published in a new section added for this purpose. After a committee reviewed Abduh's proposals, Riyad agreed to them and appointed Abduh as editor-in-chief of *Waqa'i*.[127]

On October 9, 1880, Abduh assumed his new position. Empowered with the authority to appoint a new staff, Abduh appointed Abd al-Karim Salman, Saᶜd Zaghlul—the founder of the *Wafd* (Egypt's delegation to the 1919 Paris Peace Conference which later developed into a political party) and future Prime Minister, Ibrahim al-Hilbawi, and Sayyid Wafa, as co-editors of *Waqa'i*; all were *Azhar* graduates and disciples of al-Afghani.[128] As editor in chief of *Waqa'i*, one would have expected Abduh to pursue al-Afghani's strategy of mobilizing the urban elite towards demanding the termination of Western intervention and the affirmation of Egypt's national sovereignty. Abduh, however, pursued a different course. He directed *Waqa'i* towards instilling in its readers an appreciation of the principles of Islamic reform; that is, toward the construction of a *ra'y ᶜamm* (an educated public opinion).[129]

In order to maintain his control of *Waqa'i* within the politically charged Egyptian setting of the early 1880's, Abduh was willing to identify himself, by virtue of his position as editor-in-chief of a government publication, with the Khedive who was responsible for the deportation of al-Afghani, his beloved master. He was further willing to remain loyal to Riyad Pasha, even after Riyad became the archenemy of Egypt's nationalist leaders. Finally, he would keep *Waqa'i* disengaged from the nationalist movement's rise to power until shortly prior to the British bombardment of Alexandria. In return, Abduh expected the Egyptian government to allow him to supervise *Waqa'i* in the manner he deemed appropriate. With the exception of marginal harassment by some of Urabi's followers, Abduh's control of *Waqa'i* remained unchallenged until the arrival of British soldiers in Cairo in 1882.[130]

Abduh essays in *Waqa'i*ᶜ constitute the earliest intellectual documents of the Islamic reform movement in Egypt. Al-Afghani's views, as published by a number of journals during his stay in Egypt, were not couched in Qur'anic and/or Prophetic reasoning. As noted above, he did not wish to alienate either his Christian disciples or some of his hardly religious Muslim supporters. Indeed, al-Afghani's first explicit discussions of Islamic reform are found in the articles of *al-ᶜUrwah al-Wuthqa,* published more than five years after his ouster from Egypt. Nevertheless, Abduh's articles in *Waqa'i*ᶜ indicated that al-Afghani had shared his vision of Islamic reform with him and, perhaps, with a few other Muslim disciples (e.g. Ibrahim al-Laqqani, Abd al-Karim Salman, etc.). Al-Afghani's influence may be seen in the way that three major principles of Islamic reform, 'the religious', 'the social', and 'the political', were addressed by Abduh's articles in *Waqa'i*ᶜ.

The 'purification' of Islam from *bida*ᶜ, or innovations, is at the heart of Islamic reform. A religious belief or practice is considered an innovation if it can be shown to have less than adequate authentication from the Qur'an or Prophetic traditions.[131] Innovations are not part of 'authentic Islam' and, thus, must be eliminated. The notion of *bida*ᶜ underlies the dichotomy between an 'authentic Islam' and a 'historical Islam', consistently invoked by the representatives of Islamic reform, including Abduh.[132] The strong emphasis on the 'purification' of Islam from *bida*ᶜ has been traced historically to Ibn Taymiyyah (1263-1328), responsible for a number of works, which vehemently attacked religious practices popular during his age.[133] Ibn Taymiyyah's legacy was revived by Muhammad Ibn Abd al-Wahhab (1703-1791) who, along with his followers, forcibly converted the inhabitants of Najd, and later of Hijaz, to his vision of 'pure Islam'. Abduh and Rida expressed their admiration of Abd al-Wahab's movement, though they did distance themselves from its excessive legalism and violent methods.[134]

As noted above, all government agencies, including courts, were obliged to send the editor-in-chief of *Waqa'i*ᶜ notices of their activity. Under the guise of 'a mere commentator on events', Abduh used reports and actions of certain government agencies to propagate the religious principle of Islamic reform. When he was informed during November 1880, for example, that a caretaker of one of Cairo's mosques had asked *Nazarat al-Awqaf al-ᶜUmumiyyah* (Ministry of Public Charitable Trusts) to take action against the practice of drum beating by members of *al-Tariqah al-Saᶜdiyyah* (The Saᶜdi Order), Abduh published an article in which he strongly spoke out against the practice.[135] Another complaint to *Nazarat al-Awqaf al-ᶜUmumiyyah*, during February 1881, against a popular practice known as *al-dawsah*, or the 'trampling over event', provided Abduh with an opportunity to write a series of articles in *Waqa'i*ᶜ, which further explained the religious principle of Islamic reform.[136] The practice of *al-dawsah*, which involved a Master of a spiritual order riding a horse over a road covered by a number of men lying face down, was described by Abduh as "having no identical or similar precedent in the noble Prophetic tradition."[137] To those advocating the practice, Abduh stated: "Do not the ignorant realize that Egypt, and indeed other Muslim countries, have become so permeated with harmful innovations that Islamic religious law has almost been destroyed as a result?"[138] Abduh, then, concludes with a statement destined to become the argument *par excellence* of Islamic reform: "crises have not fallen upon us and the hands of betrayal and evil did not reach us until we turned our backs on the affairs of this religion and became unconcerned with the truth of God's law."[139]

An additional principle of Islamic reform addressed by Abduh in *Waqa'i*, involved 'purifying' society of practices which could not be reconciled with Islamic precepts. Practices associated with women and marriage were among the major targets of Abduh. In a series of articles on marriage, Abduh attacked men who had contracted polygamous marriages, accusing them of sexual motivation and heedlessness of the Qur'anic emphasis on justice and equal treatment.[140] Abduh portrayed polygamy as an institution that was made permissible to perform a positive function in an exceptional situation. In the vast majority of cases, Abduh argued, polygamy causes pain and degradation to women. "How can we then allow ourselves", Abduh rhetorically asked, "to marry more than one wife for no other reason then the fulfillment of a short lived desire and the acquisition of temporal pleasure, without any concern for the harm which will occur and the violation of Islamic religious law that will be involved?"[141] Further, in a separate article on practices associated with weddings, Abduh graphically described the extent to which women were abused in wedding festivals, especially those which took place in rural areas, with specific reference to practices associated with verifying a bride's virginity.[142]

In an article entitled "*al-Shura wa al-Istibdad*" (On Constitutionalism and Authoritarianism), Abduh presented one of the earliest endorsements of constitutional government on the basis of Islamic legal authority. Abduh emphasized that each Muslim is obliged to "observe the actions of rulers, demand of them what is good and forbid them what is evil, and bring them back to true Islamic law when they stray from it."[143] This obligation, known in Islamic law as *hisbah*, is derived from a number of Qur'anic verses, Prophetic traditions and scholarly views; of which, the following are quoted by Abduh:

> "Let there be among you a group which enjoins good and forbids evil." [Qur'an, 3:104][144]

> "Religion is providing *nasihah* [good counsel]" was repeated by the Prophet three times. He was asked [by his companions] to whom [i.e. is *nasihah* to be provided]? Upon which he replied: "To...those among you in positions of authority."[145]

> The *'ulama'* stated that providing *nasihah* [good counsel] to rulers and those who have positions of authority

> must be manifested in helping them carry out their
> responsibilities, cautioning them when they are heedless,
> guiding them when they are wrong, and teaching them
> what they do not know...[146]

In Islamic cities the formal application of *hisbah* was the responsibility of the *muhtasib,* a government employee charged with policing the market.[147] As for *nasihah,* there are certain instances in Islamic history in which religious scholars acted as influential advisors to Muslim rulers. Nevertheless, their status was largely informal and did not become institutionalized. To Abduh, however, the traditional application of *hisbah* and *nasihah* was not relevant. Abduh was concerned with legitimizing constitutional government and *hisbah* and *nasihah*—with their strong emphasis on individual responsibility and active participation in the affairs of the Muslim community—were very useful in this regard. Abduh concluded his essay by attacking an article published in an Egyptian newspaper which argued that Islam does not sanction constitutional government:

> All this we have written so that we may refute the
> implication of that newspaper's article; namely, that
> our religion obligates or even permits authoritarianism,
> when, in fact, it is innocent of it. We wished further to
> make clear that the status of constitutional government
> with us Muslims is that of being an obligation, rather
> than a prohibition.[148]

The principles of Islamic reform, addressed by Abduh in *Waqa'i* were arrived at through a methodology sanctioned and practiced by *al-Azhar*; that is, the examination of Qur'anic verses, Prophetic traditions and positions held by previous religious scholars (i.e. precedents, and case studies) in order to reach a religious legal verdict on a particular issue.[149] Abduh, in his capacity as an *Azhar* graduate, employed this methodology to provide *fatawa* (plural of *fatwa* or religious verdict) on a host of issues, including, as specified above, religious practices, social relations, and forms of government. Indeed, by virtue of the circulation of *Waqa'i*, Abduh was propagating his religious legal verdicts in every city of Egypt. Not even Abbasi al-Mahdi, *Mufti al-Diyar al-Misriyyah* (the Grand Mufti of Egypt), had such a mechanism of communication at his disposal.[150] Therein lies the significance of Abduh's strategy: The use of an institution borrowed from the West, *Waqa'i*, to perform the function of a traditional institution, al-*Azhar*, under the protective mantle of an official agency of the government.

Though Abduh's use of *Waqa'i* was clearly motivated by ideological concerns, Abduh, nevertheless, had an important literary impact not only on *Waqa'i*, but on other government agencies as well.[151] Abduh demanded that correct *fusha* (Classical Arabic) be used in all government reports sent for publication in *Waqa'i*, thereby forcing government agencies to rid their reports of Turkish and *ammiyyah* (colloquial) expressions. Warnings were issued to government agencies which did not live up to Abduh's literary standards.

Between 1879 and 1882, *Waqa'i* experienced profound changes in both its content and style. Perhaps the most important aspect of these changes was the fact that they were advanced by Abduh, an *Azhar* graduate. In his *Hadith* *Isa Ibn Hisham* (The Discourse of *Isa Ibn Hisham), Muhammad al-Muwaylihi (1844-1930)—a scholar, journalist and author who was a disciple of Abduh— eloquently describes the attitude of the vast majority of *Azhar* graduates in the late nineteenth/early twentieth century towards journals and newspapers:

> Our scholars and sheikhs—may God forgive them—are of all people the least likely to...pursue the journalistic profession. They consider working in it to be heresy. They have dubbed it inquisitiveness (which the *shari*a forbids) and interference in matters of no concern to anyone. So they ignore newspapers and often disagree as to whether or not it is permissible to read them.[152]

Abduh's use of *Waqa'i*, however, was short lived. The Urabi Revolt culminating in the British bombardment of Alexandria and the subsequent British occupation of Egypt altered the situation drastically. As noted above, al-Afghani's network, which constituted the civilian branch of Egypt's nationalist movement, collapsed after al-Afghani's deportation. The military branch, embodied in Urabi and his fellow military officers, not only remained active, but became significantly stronger during the first year of Khedive Tawfiq's rule. Though united in their hostility towards the government, important differences existed between al-Afghani and Urabi. While al-Afghani, as noted, was primarily motivated by his desire to resist Western intervention and establish a constitutional government in Egypt, Urabi was primarily motivated by his desire to improve the status of Egyptian military officers in general, and that of his own in particular. Thus, one understands why Abduh perceived Urabi's rising popularity with contempt. Abduh judged Urabi's victories as having little to do with the implementation of his master's objectives. Indeed, as further explained below, Abduh believed that Urabi and his fellow army officers were creating an explosive climate which not only obstructed his utilization of *Waqa'i* for the advancement of Islamic reform, but which was also conducive to Western intervention.

On February 1, 1881, a large number of troops stormed into the War Ministry, which was housed in *Qasr al-Nil* (Palace of the Nile Barracks), and rescued Urabi and two other officers. They had been imprisoned for demanding the resignation of the minister of war, Uthman Rifqi, and the cessation of discriminatory treatment against Egyptian officers.[153] After the incident of *Qasr al-Nil*, as it came to be known, Mahmud Sami al-Barudi, a supporter of Urabi, was appointed minister of war and a number of laws were enacted in favor of Egyptian soldiers, including a substantial pay raise.[154] A week after the *Qasr al-Nil* incident Abduh published an article in *Waqa'i*, entitled "*al-Quwah wa-al-Qanun*" (Power and Law) in which he denounced the use of force to attain political objectives.

> ...let those who stray from the law and the path of order because of a momentary arrogant assessment of their increased power be merciful with themselves...[155]

On September 9, 1881, Urabi orchestrated *Muzaharat ᶜAbdin* (the ᶜAbdin Palace Demonstration) to demand the resignation of Riyad Pasha, reinstitution of the parliament and an increased number of Egyptian officers in the military.[156] After a strong show of force by Urabi, Riyad Pasha, the Prime Minister, resigned and left for Europe. Sharif Pasha, known for his constitutionalist inclinations, became the new Prime Minister.[157] It was after *Muzaharat ᶜAbdin* that Abduh wrote the previously cited articles in support of constitutional government. Although Abduh's articles were theoretical in nature, they clearly reflected a change of attitude on his part towards the nationalist movement, since only six months earlier he had characterized those who sought constitutional government as lacking in wisdom. Abduh was responding to the new realities of the political setting. Not only had Urabi become the *de facto* ruler of Egypt, but the Assembly of Delegates had also acquired an unprecedented degree of autonomy. Abduh's full identification with the nationalist movement, however, occurred only after France and England made their 'Dual Proclamation' on May 25, 1882, in which they demanded Urabi's deportation.[158] Abduh's sense of national honor, as Rida would later relate, inspired him to put aside his previous reservations and fully join the battle against the French and British attempt to impose their will on Egypt.[159]

Subsequently, Abduh became one of the most important figures of the nationalist movement, monitoring all of its major conferences, and helping compose the 'Program of the Nationalist Party in Egypt' which was translated by Wilfred Blunt, a rich Englishman sympathetic to the Egyptian national cause, and published in *The Times* of London in January 1882.[160] One of the most important functions carried out by Abduh—and the one which was later used by the post revolution tribunals to justify his deportation—was the administration of oaths. Acting on the request of Mahmud Sami al-Barudi Pasha, who replaced Sharif Pasha as Prime Minister on February 7, 1882, Abduh is said to have administered oaths to high ranking Egyptian officers, swearing them to unity and resistance to foreign intervention.[161] In choosing Abduh over a member of *al-Azhar*'s faculty, al-Barudi clearly demonstrated the significance of Abduh's position as editor-in-chief of *Waqa'i*. The committee in charge of investigating Abduh in the wake of the British invasion questioned him on this very point: "You are the editor of *al-Waqa'i* and this [i.e. the administration of oaths] is the special responsibility of *al-Azhar*. Why were you, then, chosen to carry out this task by Mahmud Sami [al-Barudi]?"[162]

Abduh responded: "Because we both were members in *Diwan al-Maᶜarif* (The Council of Education) and he knew that I am a man of knowledge and ready to obey his orders."[163] Although Abduh's reply was not inaccurate, it failed to address the question's central point, namely, by what authority was the editor-in-chief of *Waqa'iᶜ* administering such oaths?

True, Abduh was a graduate of *al-Azhar* and, thus, had the technical authority to administer oaths. Nevertheless, as pointed out by the investigative committee, it would have made more sense for al-Barudi to ask one of *al-Azhar*'s faculty to carry out this task. Unlike its role in resisting the French occupation and assisting Muhammad Ali, however, *al-Azhar*'s role in the Urabi revolt was not significant. Indeed, Muhammad al-Abbasi al-Mahdi (1827-1897), the Grand Mufti of Egypt and *Shaikh al-Azhar* (leading religious scholar of *al-Azhar*) from 1871 until December 1881, was strongly opposed to Urabi.[164] While, his successor Muhammad al-Inbabi (1824-1896) sided with Urabi, he did not actively support the revolt.[165] It was *Waqa'iᶜ*, rather, that assumed the mobilizing role that *al-Azhar* traditionally played, calling on Egypt's population to resist the British army.[166] Given these dynamics, it was not illogical for al-Barudi to turn to the editor of *Waqa'iᶜ*, rather than to the faculty of *al-Azhar*, in his attempt to endow the unity of the army officers with moral strength. Abduh was sentenced to exile for three years. As indicated by the aforementioned investigative report, his primary transgression appears to have been the administration of illegal oaths.[167] On December 24, 1882, a ship carrying Abduh and many other Egyptian deportees left Port Said and headed for Beirut.

Al-ᶜUrwah al-Wuthqah (The Firm Bond)[168]

During the same month that Abduh was transported to Beirut, al-Afghani obtained permission from the British authorities to leave India, where he had been detained since his ouster from Egypt.[169] After brief stops in Port Said and London, al-Afghani arrived in Paris on January 19, 1883, determined to undertake an intense campaign against the British occupation of Egypt. Al-Afghani's decision to make Paris the base of his anti-British campaign was not arbitrary. France was strongly against the British occupation of Egypt and, thus, willing to tolerate al-Afghani's activity on its soil. Making use of colonial rivalry was one of al-Afghani's frequently employed tactics, as is attested by accounts documenting his interaction with officials from various European countries.[170] Shortly after his arrival in Paris, al-Afghani applied for re-affiliation with Freemasonry.[171] In so doing, al-Afghani apparently hoped to meet important Masons, on whose support he hoped to rely in times of crises. However, no documents of al-Afghani's involvement with Freemasonry during his stay in France exist. Considering the volume of evidence documenting al-Afghani's involvement with Freemasonry in Egypt, it appears that the French Freemason connection—if in fact he had been admitted—was not a significant component of al-Afghani's anti-British campaign.

More importantly, al-Afghani established contact with three newspapers founded by Arab immigrants: The London-based *al-Nahlah* (The Bee), founded by Louis Sabunji, and two Paris based journals, *al-Basir* (The Aware) established by Khalil Ghanim, and *Abu Nazzarah Zarqa'* (The Man With The Blue Glasses) established by Yaqub Sannu.[172] Al-Afghani used these contacts to get a number of his anti-British articles published. *Al-Nahlah* published two of his articles: "*al-Siyasah al-Injliziyyah fi al-Mamalik al-Sharqiyyah*" (English Policy in Eastern Countries) and "*Asbab al-Harb fi Misr*" (The Reasons for the War in Egypt); *al-Basir* published three articles: "*Al-Wifaq wa-Madar al-Shiqaq*" (Reconciliation and the Harm of Conflict), "*al-Haqq wa al-Batil aw Nata'ij Siyasat al-Ingliz fi Misr*" (Truth and Falsehood or the Consequences of British Policy in Egypt), and "*al-Ingliz fi al-Hind wa Misr*" (The British in India and Egypt); *Abu Nazzarah Zarqa'* published two articles: "*Nibdhah min Munazarah Tarikhiyyah*" (An Excerpt of a Historical Debate) and "*al-Sharq wa-al-Sharqiyin*" (The East and the Easterners).[173] Al-Afghani also succeeded in getting some of his anti-British articles published in various European newspapers: *L'Intransigeant* published a translation of "*al-Ingliz fi al-Hind wa Misr*" and a translation of "*al-Haqq wa al-Batil aw Nata'ij Siyasat al-Ingliz fi Misr*".[174] Further, al-Afghani published articles in European newspapers which did not have an earlier Arabic version, including his famous "Réponse a Renan" (Response to Renan), published in *Journal des Debats,* and three other articles in *L'Intransigeant.*[175]

Abduh reestablished contact with al-Afghani after his arrival in Beirut.[176] Though there is no documentation of al-Afghani's response, Abduh's subsequent arrival in Paris, early in 1884, suggests that al-Afghani had, indeed, responded, inviting Abduh to join him in Paris. The expenses covering Abduh's trip seem to have been obtained by al-Afghani from the ex-Khedive Ismail. On March 13, 1884, the first issue of *ᶜUrwah* appeared. Information published in *ᶜUrwah* came from a large array of sources, including French and English newspapers, and influential English government officials. French newspapers utilized by *ᶜUrwah* included, *République Francaise, Matin,* and *Debat.* English newspapers included, *Daily News, Daily Telegraph, Morning Press, Pall Mall Gazette, Post, Standard,* and *The Times.*[177] Information utilized from these newspapers was translated by several paid interpreters.[178] Mirza Muhammad Baqir Bavanati and Yaqub Sannu also helped al-Afghani obtain information from European newspapers.[179] Further, Ibrahim al-Muwaylihi and his son Muhammad seem to have played a role in the publication of *ᶜUrwah,* though it is not clear whether or not either one actually wrote any of its articles.[180]

ᶜUrwah was sent free of charge to political leaders, religious scholars and influential figures in various Muslim countries. A notebook, cataloged in *Documents* and preserved at the *Library of Parliament in Teheran*, contains detailed information on the names of the figures *ᶜUrwah* was sent to and the number of issues each country received. (See Table 2)

Table 2: *ᶜUrwah*'s Circulation[181]

Total Number of Issues Sent to Egypt: (551)
Known Recipients:
- The immediate entourage of the Khedive
- Riyad Pasha
- Sharif Pasha
- Abd al-Salam al-Muwaylihi, a disciple of al-Afghani
- Four unnamed *Azhar* professors
- Publishers of the following journals: *Mir'at al-Sharq, al-Bayan,* and *al-Watan*

Total Number of Issues Sent to Istanbul: (88)
Known Recipients:
- Sultan Abd al-Hamid
- Munif Pasha, an associate of al-Afghani in Istanbul
- Khair al-Din Pasha, a Tunisian reformer
- Abu al-Huda al-Sayyadi, the Sultan's religious advisor
- Muᶜin al-Mulk, the Iranian Ambassador in Istanbul
- Ismail Jawdat, Cairo's Chief of Police under Khedive Ismail
- Publishers of the following journals: *al-Jawa'ib* and *al-Iᶜtidal*

Total Number of Issues Sent to Beirut (114 issues)
Total Number of Issues Sent to Tripoli (11 issues)
Total Number of Issues Sent to Damascus (23 issues)
Total Number of Issues Sent to Baghdad (7 issues)
Total Number of Issues Sent to Mecca (5 issues)
Total Number of Issues Sent to Madinah (2 issues)
Total Number of Issues Sent to North Africa (20 issues)
Iran (?)[182]/ India (?)[183]/ Indonesia (?)[184]/ Ceylon (?)[185]

Al-Afghani seems to have also arranged for several articles of *ᶜUrwah to* be translated into Persian and published in Iranian newspapers, including *Farhang, Akhbar-e ᶜAm* and *Itlaᶜ*. Further, a number of articles were translated into Urdu and published in Indian newspapers, including *Udah Akhbar* and *Bazar Partarka*, thereby bringing *ᶜUrwah*'s message to a wider audience.[186]

In their totality, documents involving fund raising by al-Afghani and Abduh until late in 1884, indicate that funds were sought and frequently obtained from various influential and wealthy figures. Some contributors included, Prince Abd al-Halim, the ex-Khedive Ismail, Husain Pasha, an associate of the Tunisian reformer Khair al-Din al-Tunisi who had migrated to Italy after the establishment of the French protectorate, Ahmad Pasha al-Minshawi, a rich Egyptian nationalist, and Wilfred Blunt.[187] Al-Afghani's success in obtaining funds from these figures was rooted in his capacity to turn their personal aspirations toward his own advantage. Both Abd al-Halim and Ismail were very much interested in destabilizing the British presence in Egypt. They seem to have reasoned that a British withdrawal would discredit Tawfiq and, thus, force the European powers to designate a new Khedive. Husain, al-Minshawi and Blunt, on the other hand, appear to have been motivated by a certain degree of genuine respect for the views and activities of al-Afghani and Abduh. In October 1884, only seven months after its first issue appeared, *ᶜUrwah*'s publication terminated because of lack of sufficient funds, owing to the decision of its major financiers to cease their support.[188] *ᶜUrwah*'s highly politicized content appears to have alarmed Ismail and alienated Blunt. While, Ismail's alarm is exhibited by his unexplained refusal to continue his support, Blunt's alienation is evident in the following statement he allegedly made to al-Afghani: "It is impossible for me to finance a newspaper hostile to my country."[189]

The opening article of *ᶜUrwah* affirmed that a number of rational men had responded to the Western challenge by creating *ᶜisabat*, groupings or associations.[190] These associations are said to have been located in "many Muslim countries, especially India and Egypt."[191] The article goes on to say that representatives of these associations had met in Mecca and called for the foundation of an Arabic newspaper in Paris, so that it could act as the vehicle through which their views would be disseminated throughout the world. Jamal al-Din al-Afghani, the article continues, was asked by these representatives to carry out this task on their behalf. Al-Afghani accepted and asked, in turn, Muhammad Abduh to be the newspaper's editor. The notion of *ᶜUrwah* associations, however, was little more than a means used by al-Afghani and Abduh to endow *ᶜUrwah*, the journal, with an aura of significance and, more importantly, facilitate fund-raising.

Two months after *ᶜUrwah*'s last issue, Abduh traveled to Tunis in an attempt to obtain funds which would allow the re-publication of *ᶜUrwah*. On December 24, 1884, he sent a letter from Tunis to al-Afghani in Paris describing the outcome of his visit. Abduh stated that he had informed the religious scholars he had met that *ᶜUrwah* was not only the name of a newspaper, but also the name of an association which al-Afghani had founded in Hyderabad, India which had branches in many Muslim countries. Abduh also reported that after explaining to the Tunisian religious scholars the need to form a branch of the association in Tunis, a branch was formed. Abduh noted that the persons he met in Tunis were unaware of the termination of *ᶜUrwah*'s publication and concluded by stating that he had failed, as yet, to raise any funds.[192] Rida includes in his biography of Abduh two documents pertaining to *al-ᶜUqd al-Rabiᶜ Li-Jamᶜi-yyat al-ᶜUrwah al-Wuthqah* (The Fourth Branch of the Association of the Firm Bond). While, the first contains an oath, seemingly based on a Masonic model, which members of this branch had to swear upon joining, the second contains the regulations governing the activities of this branch. The latter document may be paraphrased as follows:

(1)   Three members are to be present at all sessions.

(2)   Each session begins with a recitation of the oath formula.[193]

(3)   Members are to seek answers on why Muslims have declined by reflecting on themselves.

(4)   Members are to reflect on resisting their invaders.

(5)   Members are to reflect on the present conditions of Muslims.

(6)   Ideas are to be discussed and solutions are to be proposed.

(7-8)   Members are to utilize all types of methods to apply literary, economic and military solutions.

(9-14) Intense recruitment of new members is to be pursued.

(15-17) Unless unable, each new member is required to pay at least 100 francs in dues. Members are to meet twice a week. At each meeting, financial contributions are to be made.

(18-19) All funds are to be kept by the treasurer.

(20)   Funds are to be used for the expenses of renting a place for the branch's sessions and recruitment. What remains of the funds is to be sent to the main branch of the association in Paris.

(21)   The branch is to have four types of records: membership, recruitment offices, and expenses.

(22)   If large funds are collected, members of the branch should try to invest it properly.

(23)   Records of the funds are to be kept by the branch.

(24)   No funds are to be used without the agreement of the majority of the branch's members.

(25)   Funds for urgent situations are to be collected as needed.

(26)   All members should be committed to complete secrecy in regard to their branch.

(27-28) Members are obliged to protect one another to their full capacity.

(29)   New regulations must be sanctioned by the major branch.

(30)   Regulations involving conduct during meetings are to be made by members of the branch.[194]

Since no documentation exists of any 'first', 'second', or 'third' branch of the *Urwah* association, it appears that the above paraphrased regulations are the very regulations of the branch created by Abduh in Tunis. That Rida found these regulations, along with the oath of entry, among Abduh's papers (and nowhere else) further documents their exclusive Tunisian link.[195] As can be seen, the bulk of the regulations (9-25) address financial concerns. Thus, it becomes clear why Abduh created this singular real branch of his fictitious association, namely, to recruit Tunisian religious scholars into an institution which obligated them to pay not only membership fees but to make continuous other financial contributions as well.

In *cUrwah*, al-Afghani reproduced his Egyptian discourse in terms of Qur'anic and Prophetic terminology and reasoning. It is therefore not surprising that Salim al-Anhuri, a Christian disciple of al-Afghani in Egypt, regarded *cUrwah* as constituting a change of course by al-Afghani.[196] As noted above, al-Afghani's arguments in Egypt were sensitive to his Christian and non-committed Muslim disciples. When al-Afghani sought to mobilize the Egyptians against Khedive Ismail and Western intervention, he appealed to their Egyptian national identity. In *cUrwah*, on the other hand, al-Afghani, like Abduh, consistently invoked the *ummah*, or the Global Community of Muslims, revealing in the process the 'unity principle' of Islamic reform.

> ...unity and seeking victory, are strong pillars and firm cornerstones of Islam. They are also categorical obligations.[197]

The *cUrwah* experience confirmed the power embodied in the print media. Indeed, al-Afghani fully understood that mobilization was a function of the availability of information. Thus, for example, we find him preoccupied with informing Muslims in India of al-Mahdi's victories over General Gordon in Sudan.[198] In one of *cUrwah*'s articles, he writes:

> The British want to obstruct Muslims from going on pilgrimage this year, and maybe even next year as well, in order that they may prevent news of Muhammad Ahmad [i.e. al-Mahdi] and the difficulties the British are experiencing in fighting him from reaching the ears of the Indians...[199]

Indeed, thanks to *cUrwah*'s distribution in India, Indian Muslims did not have to depend on the return of pilgrims to learn of events in Sudan.[200]

We have seen how information dissemination was one of the fundamental components of *al-Azhar*'s strategy in mobilizing resistance against Napoleon's troops. Prior to Cairo's first insurrection, news of the British defeat of the French navy and of approaching Ottoman forces had been extensively circulated by *Azhar* scholars through their connections with the spiritual orders, despite French orders to the contrary.[201] Likewise, al-Afghani paved the path towards rebellion against the British by circulating information which encouraged the mass mobilization of anti-British opinion. Unlike *al-Azhar*, however, al-Afghani had no links to institutions like the spiritual orders which could have been organized to act upon the information made available to them through *ᶜUrwah*. Significantly, the sole rebellion against colonialism attributed to *ᶜUrwah* occurred in Tunisia, the only Muslim country where an actual *ᶜUrwah* association existed.[202] The primary movers behind the Tunisian rebellion of April 2, 1885 against the French protectorate were members of the *ᶜUrwah* 'branch' established by Abduh. The rebellion, however, failed to achieve its objectives and was short-lived. After late 1885, the Tunisian *ᶜUrwah* branch ceased to exist.[203]

Despite its failure to achieve its objectives, *ᶜUrwah* was by no means a fruitless project. It succeeded in converting a large number of religious scholars to the Afghani/Abduh vision of Islamic reform, most notable of whom was Rashid Rida. On his encounter with *ᶜUrwah*, Rida wrote:

> It, then, happened that I was browsing through the papers of my father...when I came across two issues of *al-ᶜUrwah al-Wuthqah*. So I read them with eagerness and joy...I searched for the remaining issues and found some with my father and the rest with my teacher al-Shaikh Husain al-Jisr al-Tarabulsi. I copied them all and read them again and again and was carried, as a result, to a new understanding of Islam.[204]

Shortly after Abduh returned to Paris from Tunisia, he was sent by al-Afghani on another mission to establish contact with al-Mahdi.[205] As indicated by correspondence between Abduh and some of the Tunisian religious scholars, Abduh, en route to Sudan, entered Egypt secretly, but the sudden death of al-Mahdi in June 1885, aborted simultaneously al-Afghani's plans and Abduh's mission. Abduh then traveled to Beirut, arriving late in 1885.

Al-Manar (The Beacon)

After receiving a pardon from Khedive Tawfiq in 1888, Abduh returned to Egypt. There he was faced with two major questions, how to react to the British occupation, and by what institutional means should he advance Islamic reform? Abduh's conceptual response to the British occupation is clearly articulated in an article, dated April 1892, which he wrote for a London based Arabic journal called *Diya' al-Khafiqayn* (Light of The Two Hemispheres).[206] Abduh wrote:

> The fact of the matter is that the acquisition of the freedom which we currently enjoy and the introduction of reforms has not been realized, except through the agency of the British and no one else...Were it not for the British army our rulers would not have submitted to the implementation of reforms.[207]

Thus, Abduh concluded, the evacuation of the British forces must be postponed until "the appropriate time, since the achievement of all goals is dependent on the arrival of the appropriate moment."[208] Abduh, in short, advocated the use of the British occupation to advance internal reforms which the Khedive and his government would have normally opposed.

In 1895, Abduh was appointed a member of *al-Azhar*'s administrative council. Through this position of authority, he introduced several administrative reforms, especially of finances, which he hoped would result in the restoration of *al-Azhar*'s autonomy from government authority, thereby paving the way for it to play a role in the advancement of Islamic reform.[209] In the words of Rida, Abduh's objective was to "establish the legal and administrative autonomy of *al-Azhar*'s *ᶜulama'* in order to create a condition in which the government could no longer control *al-Azhar*, and the Khedive could no longer play [games] with it."[210] Abduh's attempts at reforming *al-Azhar*, however, were consistently aborted by both Khedive Tawfiq and his successor, Khedive Abbas Hilmi.[211] Abduh's resignation from *al-Azhar*'s administrative council shortly prior to his death in 1905 reflected his deep frustration and failure to bring about significant change in *al-Azhar*'s relationship with the government.[212] At the same time, Abduh's resignation reflected a sense of confidence in the capacity of *Manar,* a journal founded seven years earlier, to perform the task *al-Azhar* refused to assume.[213]

Muhammad Rashid Rida (1865-1935) was born in Tripoli, Ottoman Syria, into a religious *Sunni* family.[214] At a young age, he was initiated into *al-Tariqah al-Naqshbandiyyah* (The Naqshbandi Order), and became deeply involved in sufism. He received a traditional education at *al-Madrasah al-Islamiyyah* (The Islamic School), founded by Husain al-Jisr al-Tarabulsi and completed his studies in 1896. Although Rida never met al-Afghani, it was al-Afghani's words, as he encountered them in *ᶜUrwah,* that transformed him into a firm believer in the vision of Islamic reform. Eager to meet the man responsible for his new convictions, Rida wrote to al-Afghani, pledging his loyalty and offering his services. Al-Afghani at the time, however, was in Istanbul under the constant surveillance of Abd al-Hamid's spies. When Rida learned of al-Afghani's death in 1897, he decided to join Abduh whom he viewed as al-Afghani's primary disciple. Rida arrived in Cairo on January 18, 1898. After a month of constant visits to Abduh's house, Rida proposed the establishment of a newspaper to advance the principles of Islamic reform.[215] Abduh was initially hesitant, citing the large number of newspapers and journals already published in Egypt.[216] At a subsequent meeting, Rida brought up the idea again, whereupon Abduh expressed his skepticism about the effectiveness of the written word. Abduh, according to Rida, said:

> Oral discourse has a stronger impact on the soul than
> does written discourse...the listener understands eighty
> percent of what the speaker wishes to convey, while the

reader understands only twenty percent of what the writer wished to convey.[217]

Rida responded as follows:

> Many figures in various countries are aware of the character of this age and accurately understand Islam. Most of these persons were not awakened [to this understanding] except by *al-ʿUrwah al-Wuthqah.* Indeed, I did not become enlightened about that of which I am now aware of except through it [i.e. *ʿUrwah*].[218]

Recalling Abduh's previous involvement in *Waqaʾiʿ* and *ʿUrwah*, it is difficult to take seriously his emphasis on the superiority of oral discourse. Abduh appears, rather, to have been testing Rida's commitment to the newspaper project. Indeed, Rida's strong response succeeded in winning Abduh's approval and promise of cooperation. On March 15, 1898, the first edition of *Manar*, Cairo's first Islamic reform newspaper, appeared. Abduh used his contacts to obtain a printing press.[219] In regard to funding, the evidence indicates that Rida initially depended on his own savings and, subsequently, on *Manar*'s subscribers, since, unlike *ʿUrwah, Manar* was not distributed free of cost.[220] The only documented occasion of external funding involves a loan from one of Abduh's associates, which Rida obtained in 1901 after *Manar*'s administrative office was burglarized.[221]

Manar was initially published on a weekly basis in the format of a newspaper.[222] In its second year, it was changed into a monthly journal. According to Rida, the change was made in response to the request of some of *Mana*r's subscribers who complained that their desire to bind *Manar*'s issues was inhibited by its large pages; financial factors, however, may have also been involved.[223] Judging by its almost immediate appearance in India and Tunisia, Abduh apparently provided Rida with *ʿUrwah*'s mailing list. Fifteen hundred copies of each issue were printed during the first year. Copies were sent to various personalities in Egypt, Syria, and many other Muslim countries.[224] While, the vast majority of copies sent to Syria were intercepted and confiscated by the Ottoman authorities, the majority of Egyptians, to whom *Manar was* sent with the hope of gaining subscriptions, returned *Manar* to Rida.[225] Though Rida does not explain why *Manar* was initially turned down in Egypt, it appears that the popularity of a journal in Egypt during the late nineteenth century was significantly a function of its association with a known faction or personality. Rida, however, was an unknown Syrian whose connection with Abduh was not yet widely known.

Manar's circulation experienced a dramatic increase during its fifth year (1903).[226] Abduh, who supported *Manar* from its inception, appears to have been largely responsible for its increased popularity. According to Rida, Abduh allowed, and at times encouraged, others to identify *Manar* as the purveyor of

Table 3: *Manar's* Circulation By Country, As Indicated By the National Origins of Letters Requesting Religious Legal Verdicts* [232]

Year	Country
1903:	Sudan, Algeria, Bahrain, Lebanon, Serbia & Montenegro
1904:	Yemen, America, Bosnia & Herzegovina, Syria, Tunis
1905:	Malaysia, India, Pakistan
1906:	Singapore
1907:	Saudi Arabia, Uzbekistan
1909:	Iraq, Argentina, Indonesia
1910:	Turkey, Ceylon
1912:	Oman, South Africa
1913:	United Kingdom, Iran
1914:	Kuwait
1922:	Tanzania
1927:	Uganda
1928:	Switzerland
1929:	United Arab Emirates
1930:	Thailand
1931:	Brazil
1933:	Germany[233]

his views, thereby, legitimizing its claim to be the literary expression of Islamic reform.[227] Further, Abduh's frequent praise of *Manar*'s content endowed it with " acceptance and respect from the highest social classes in Egypt."[228] *Manar*'s publication of essays by Abduh written in response to controversial articles by Farah Antun in *al-Jami'ah,* seems to have played an important 'attention-capturing' role.[229] Ironically, it was Abduh's death which ultimately established *Manar* as one of the most influential Arabic journals of its age.[230] *Manar*, by virtue of its consistent commitment to Abduh's views, satisfied the thirst of those who wanted to maintain some type of connection with Abduh after his death. By its twelfth year, 1910, issues of *Manar*'s early years were being compiled and bound into volumes and sold for four times their original price.[231] The extent of *Manar*'s circulation is indicated in its '*Fatawa*' section, discussed further below. Letters sent to this section show *Manar to* have far exceeded *ᶜUrwah*'s breadth of circulation. (See Table 3)

Abduh's willingness to identify himself with *Manar* had three major conditions:

- That we do not incline towards any of the existing political factions [in Egypt]...
- That we do not respond to the hostile remarks or criticism of any journal.
- That we do not serve the objectives of any influential figure...[234]

Abduh's conditions shaped *Manar*'s strategy. The objective of these conditions was to prevent the newly born journal from becoming a tool of one of Egypt's competing political factions, and to protect it from becoming part of a conflict which would result in its termination. Having been assured, Abduh proceeded to help Rida make of *Manar* the mouthpiece of Islamic reform.

Manar's discourse was expressed in three major genres, '*Tafsir*' (Qur'anic Exegeses), '*Fatawa*' (Religious Legal Rulings), and '*Tarbiyah*' (Moral Guidance and Education). In his introduction to *Tafsir al-Manar* (*Manar*'s Qur'anic Exegesis)—a twelve volume compilation of *Manar*'s sections on Qur'anic exegeses—Rida recounts that even before he spoke to Abduh about the idea of creating a journal, he proposed to him the writing of an entire exegesis of the Qur'an.[235] Abduh, however, was not convinced of the necessity of such a project.[236] In June 1900, approximately fifteen months after *Manar*'s first issue appeared, Abduh agreed to a compromise proposal regarding Rida's request, namely, rather than writing a work of exegesis, Abduh would give lectures on the Qur'an at *al-Azhar*.[237] *Manar* began to publish Abduh's lectures shortly after they began.[238] Even after Abduh's death in 1905, Rida continued, until May 15, 1912, to publish notes he had taken during Abduh's lectures.[239] Rida, subsequently, proceeded to share his own Qur'anic exegesis which continued until his death in 1935. While Abduh's exegesis begins with 'Sura I, Verse: 1' and ends at 'Sura: IV, Verse: 126', Rida's begins at the point Abduh left off and ends at 'Sura: XII, Verse: 101'.[240] *Manar*'s exegesis covered various principles of Islamic reform, including those previously addressed by *Waqa'iᶜ* and *ᶜUrwah*. One of its distinct themes, however, was its emphasis on the role of reason in understanding the Qur'an, articulating, in the process, the 'rational' principle of Islamic reform which gave the movement its modern tone.[241] In speaking of the Qur'anic stand on the utilization of reason, for example, one reads in *Manor*'s exegesis:

> Thus, the Qur'an took the position of strongly emphasizing the use of reason and analytical reflection. Indeed, one hardly reads any part of the Qur'an without having the universe revealed, along with the commandment to reflect upon it and unearth its secrets and identify the principles

> underlying its constants and variables: 'Reflect upon
> what is in the heavens and the earth' (10:101); 'Travel in
> the Earth and reflect upon how He began creation'…in
> addition to many other verses.[242]

In articulating the 'rational' principle of Islamic reform, Abduh hoped to achieve two major objectives. First, Abduh hoped to affirm the right of religious scholars to practice *ijtihad*; that is, the formulation of new religious legal verdicts. Though *Sunni* Islam had no official religious body such as a synod or council which could deny the religious scholar the right of *ijtihad*, a hostile attitude towards *ijtihad* had been harbored by *Sunni* religious scholars from as early as the twelfth century.[243] Second, Abduh hoped to demonstrate that Islam and reason were not opposing camps. On the contrary, Islam had the capacity to embrace new scientific discoveries and technological developments.

On June 3, 1899, fifteen months after *Manar* was born, Abduh was appointed the Grand Mufti of Egypt. Since religious legal verdicts made by the Grand Mufti were not made known to the community at large, but, rather, confined to the works of *fiqh* (Islamic jurisprudence) and government files, the position was largely symbolic.[244] Rida, however, seized the opportunity and began to publish Abduh's verdicts in *Manar*, thereby endowing them with unprecedented influence.[245] Beginning with October 10, 1904, a formal section entitled '*al-Fatawa*' was added to *Manar.*[246] While Abduh was largely responsible for providing the verdicts which appeared in this section until his death (June 11, 1905), Rida—who, as previously noted, was also trained as a religious scholar—was responsible for the verdicts which appeared subsequently; a total of five hundred and ten.[247] *Manar*'s verdicts dealt with numerous issues, including the wearing of European hats, trust funds, perfumes containing alcohol, the shape of the earth, and smoking during the recitation of the Qur'an.[248]

One year prior to his death, Rida wrote several essays in *Manar* which he compiled and published under the heading *al-Manar wa-al-Azhar* (*Manar and al-Azhar*). The work is clearly the most important document regarding the journalistic activity of Islamic reform. Written at the height of *Manar*'s popularity, *al-Manar wa-al-Azhar* constituted a declaration of the reform movement's victory in establishing a religious scholarly authority independent of that of the religious college. The work portrays *al-Azhar* as an institution which ceased to play an important role in the community after losing its financial and administrative autonomy to government authority.[249] Beginning with al-Afghani, representatives of Islamic reform had tried to restore to *al-Azhar* its previous independence from government influence.[250] Its faculty, paid by the government, resisted such attempts. Thus, *Manar* was founded to carry out the task which *al-Azhar* rejected.[251] Indeed, as pointed out by Rida, *al-Azhar* had lost its administrative and financial autonomy to the government. *Manar*'s successful avoidance of the same fate, however, was due to British protection. It was Abduh's positive relationship with Cromer and, subsequently, Rida's positive relationship with Cromer's successors, that protected *Manar* from a number of documented attempts by the government to influence its content or suppress it altogether.[252] In his collected essays, Rida further related that in 1928, a loyal student of Abduh, Muhammad Mustafa al-Maraghi (d. 1945), became Head of *al-Azhar*.[253] Even al-Maraghi's attempts at reforming *al-Azhar*'s relationship with the government were resisted, causing him to resign a year after he assumed his position.[254] Al-Maraghi was replaced by Muhammad Ahmadi al-Zawahiri (d. 1944) who, in addition to being eager to please the government, began an intense campaign against Islamic reform through *Nur al-Islam* (The Light of Islam), a journal he founded for this purpose.[255] *Al-Manar wa-al-Azhar,* Rida emphasized, was not a response to *Nur al-Islam*. The work, rather, as indicated by both its title and content, was a response by *Manar* to *al-Azhar*'s anti-reform position. Rida clearly considered *Nur al-Islam* to be unworthy of such a response.

Rida's assessment of *Manar* was not exaggerated. *Manar*, after all, addressed the very religious sciences taught at *al-Azhar*. In a sense, subscribing to *Manar* was much like enrolling in a virtual religious college which, as indicated by the extent of its distribution, embraced students as far east as Indonesia and as far west as America. Each time a verdict was sought from Rida, *Manar*'s claim to an authority parallel with, indeed superior to, that of *al-Azhar* was endowed with legitimacy. Even some of *al-Azhar*'s students were students of *Manar*.[256] Under al-Zawahiri's management of *al-Azhar*, however, support of *Manar*'s views by faculty members or students was sufficient grounds for dismissal.[257] It was no accident that Rida ended *al-Manar wa-al-Azhar* with ten pages full of Qur'anic verses, Prophetic traditions, and scholarly statements prohibiting befriending, and establishing close relationships with unjust rulers, especially by religious scholars.[258] The co-opting of *al-Azhar*'s faculty by government authority was a major incentive for the creation of *Manar*, an institution which belonged to the realm of Muslim civil society. Indeed, the seeds earlier planted by al-Afghani vividly bloomed in *Manar*.

Chapter 4

Associations

The reform movement's involvement with associations began during al-Afghani's stay in Egypt (1871-1879). The associations inspired by al-Afghani, however, terminated following the British occupation in 1882. The ᶜUrwah association, as previously explained, existed only in Tunis and terminated shortly after its inception. It was during Abduh's stay in Beirut (1886) that the reform movement's serious involvement with associations would begin.

From 1886 and until the early twentieth century, a large number of benevolent associations were inspired by Abduh and, later, Rida. From around 1907 and until the 1920s, Rida became involved with three major political associations; the first aimed at securing Arab autonomy within the framework of the Ottoman empire, the second, aimed at achieving Arab independence from the Ottoman empire, and the third, aimed at terminating the European mandate over Syria and Lebanon. From 1927 and until the late 1930s, various youth associations were inspired by Rida in Egypt and other Muslim countries which aimed at recruiting the educated youth to the Islamic reform movement. Though initially a synthesis between a benevolent and a youth association, *al-Ikhwan al-Muslimun* (The Muslim Brotherhood) emerged in 1939 as the reform movement's first political party in Egypt.[259] By 1948, *Ikhwan* claimed over one hundred thousand members and numerous branches throughout Egypt. Not since the early nineteenth century had Islam and popular political activism been so strongly intertwined in Egypt. Its subsequent sponsoring of a paramilitary unit, however, proved to be a fatal flaw. Indeed, the political violence sponsored by this paramilitary unit was destined to trigger the collapse of the civil society that the Islamic reform movement strived so hard to create.

Benevolent Associations

The benevolent association, as it emerged in late nineteenth century Egypt, was an institution organized to enable a small group of individuals to provide free charitable services to the community, usually involving education or relief aid.[260] The association relied on private fund raising to finance its projects. Decisions regarding which projects would be sponsored by the association and how collected funds will be invested were generally made by a committee of trustees.

Abduh was first introduced to benevolent associations by al-Afghani who, during his stay in Egypt, inspired Abd Allah al-Nadim to found *al-Jamᶜiyyah al-Khayriyyah al-Islamiyyah* (The Islamic Benevolent Association) in 1878.[261] Abduh was so impressed by the institution that he published an article in *Waqa'iᶜ,* praising the type of activity sponsored by the benevolent association and thanking the Egyptian government for sanctioning the creation of such an institution.[262] During his stay in Beirut, Abduh was asked to teach at one of the schools sponsored by *Jamᶜiyyat al-Maqasid al-Islamiyyah* (Islamic Association of Noble Aspirations) founded in 1880 under the sponsorship of the famous Ottoman reformer Midhat Pasha.[263] Abduh accepted and, as indicated by a number of accounts, successfully utilized his position to infuse the institution with reformist principles.[264] Among Abduh's students was Shakib Arslan, a Druze notable who later became one of the reform movement's most important activists.[265] In 1892, six years after he returned to Egypt, Abduh and a number of his supporters founded *al-Jamᶜiyyah al-Khayriyyah al-Islamiyyah* (the Islamic Benevolent Association).[266] The institution was highly successful in establishing schools for Muslim youth and raising funds to assist communities which had experienced natural disasters.[267] Schools sponsored by *al-Jamᶜiyyah al-Khayriyyah al-Islamiyyah* stressed the 'rational' principle of Islamic reform; that is, the compatibility of Islam with new scientific discoveries and technological developments.[268]

Al-Jamᶜiyyah al-Khayriyyah al-Islamiyyah inspired imitations elsewhere in the Muslim world. During his studies at *al-Azhar*, Shubli al-Numani, an Indian religious scholar, met Abduh and became, as a result, a strong supporter of the Islamic reform movement. After he returned to India in 1894, he proceeded to infuse *Nadwat al-ᶜUlama'* (The Forum of Religious Scholars), an institution founded for the purpose of introducing Western sciences to Muslim youth, with reformist principles.[269] In 1896, *al-Jamᶜiyyah al-Khalduniyyah* (The Khalduniyyah Association) an institution similar to *Nadwat al-ᶜUlama'*, was founded in Tunisia under the patronage of French authorities who hoped to use it to advocate Western thought and science among students of religious colleges. Tunisian religious scholars who agreed to participate in the activity of *al-Jamᶜiyyah al-Khalduniyyah* were deeply committed to Abduh's ideas and, thus, placed much emphasis on his reformist principles.[270]

Rida utilized *Manar* not only to advance reformist principles, but also to advance reformist institutions. In an essay entitled *Positive and Negative Aspects Pertaining to the Presence of Europeans in the East*, for example, Rida writes:

> ...associations are the primary reason for every type of superior development. It is by means of associations that...governments in Europe were reformed and sciences and arts were significantly developed...Now we see the East is learning from the West how to create associations and companies. While, the nation of Japan has succeeded in this endeavor, the Ottoman nation and the Egyptians remain in the stage of infancy as regards this communal cooperative life...[271]

True to his words, Rida played an important role in the rise of a number of benevolent associations. Thus, we find him touring Egypt to help open various branches of *Jamʿiyyat Shams al-Islam* (The Association of the Sun of Islam), founded by Abduh supporters in 1899. We further find Rida consistently praising in *Manar* the various benevolent activities sponsored by this association, which included the creation of schools in Egyptian villages.[272] In 1909, four years after Abduh's death, Rida created *Jamʿiyyat al-Daʿwah wa-al-Irshad* (The Association for the Propagation [i.e. of Islam] and Guidance) which was meant to train a number of Muslim youth in Islamic missionary activity. The beginning of World War I, however, caused a dramatic increase in prices, making Rida's attempt to sustain the activity of *Jamʿiyyat al-Daʿwah wa-al-Irshad* in addition to *Manar* very difficult. Thus, the activity of the association terminated late in 1914.[273] Rida visited Ottoman Syria immediately after the coup engineered by the Committee of Union and Progress (C.U.P.) in 1908 and the reinstitution of the constitution. There, he found no active benevolent associations. Both *al-Jamʿiyyah al-Khayriyyah al-Islamiyyah* (The Islamic Benevolent Association) of Damascus and the previously noted *Jamʿiyyat al-Maqasid al-Khayriyyah* of Beirut which were founded during Midhat Pasha's administration had been taken over by *Majlis al-Maʿarif* (The Council of Education), a government agency, as part of Abd al-Hamid's anti-reformist policies.[274] In his account of his trip, published in *Manar,* Rida related the type of advice he shared with the religious scholars of Damascus.

> ...and I would then proceed to make clear the necessity of ensuring that schools are founded for spreading private education among all classes of the community. Indeed, such schools are dependent on the creation of benevolent associations in every administrative unit of each province...[275]

Rida also related that during a lesson he gave in *al-Jami^c al-Umawi* (the Ummayyad Mosque) of Damascus, he addressed the necessity of establishing private schools to integrate the sciences of Islam with Western sciences. He again emphasized that "such schools can only be properly cared for by benevolent associations."[276] Rida's emphasis on private education, as he himself once explained, was grounded, in his strong distrust of government sponsored education:

> Indeed, guidance and education belong to a very important realm that should be delegated to associations. It is not appropriate to leave this activity to...governments. This is so because...governments seek only workers who resemble machines, having no will, no opinion and no autonomy.[277]

Rida's efforts towards the creation of benevolent associations in Ottoman Syria went beyond mere advice. Rida relates that he personally asked the Grand Mufti of Tripoli, the city in which he was born and raised, to "create a benevolent Islamic association like that of Egypt."[278] Rida adds that he pleaded with the Grand Mufti to invite the notables of Tripoli that he may ask them to help create such an institution. Though the Grand Mufti was not initially enthusiastic about the idea, he eventually conceded. To an audience of more than twenty notables, Rida delivered a speech on the merits of benevolent associations. Sensing the positive reception of his words, Rida elicited financial pledges from the audience. Rida's efforts laid the cornerstone of the benevolent association created in Tripoli shortly after he returned to Egypt.[279] In addition to his relationship with Egyptian and Syrian benevolent associations, Rida also maintained close ties with both *al-Jam^ciyyah Khalduniyyah* and *Nadwat al-^cUlama*. In response to an invitation from the latter, he visited India in 1913, and lectured in a number of Indian cities.[280]

Abduh's primary advice to reformist benevolent associations was that they should concentrate on education and refrain from becoming involved in politics. In a letter addressed to an Algerian religious scholar, Abd al-Hamid Samayyah, Abduh wrote:

> ...I find it very necessary to explicitly warn you from becoming preoccupied with addressing or discussing your government's policy, or any other government's policy for that matter. Indeed, this dangerous activity may bring about harm quickly. People, rather, are in need of the light of knowledge and of sincerity in action...[281]

Abduh's advice to benevolent associations is better understood when placed in the larger context of the overall intellectual development of the Islamic reform movement. Abduh's separation from Afghani following the termination of *ᶜUrwah*'s publication, marked the beginning of a new conceptual approach to Islamic reform. Twice Abduh had watched his master's plans fail; in Egypt where al-Afghani's network was destroyed overnight, and in Paris, where *ᶜUrwah* terminated without achieving any of its declared objectives. He emerged from these experiences convinced that a more gradual, indirect, and community oriented approach to Islamic reform must be pursued by Muslim reformers.[282] Abduh's advice against political involvement, however, addressed a particular manifestation of politics, namely, the direct confrontation of government authority. Abduh was by no means condemning all types of political activity. Indeed, Abduh's very advice to benevolent associations was highly political since it implied that the best strategy to overcome Western colonialism and authoritarian governments was through infusing the new generation with the principles of Islamic reform. Rida eloquently identifies the political implications of Abduh's approach to Islamic reform as follows: "[Abduh sought] the reform of the government through the reform of the community."[283]

Political Associations

The term 'political association' is used here to denote political institutions which, unlike political parties, did not operate in a parliamentary climate, that is, they had no access to popular elections. These institutions were marked by the distinct character of their leaders, i.e. elitist, the restrictions they frequently imposed on who could join them, especially in the case of the institutions treated below, and their reliance on mobilization, i.e. of Muslim rulers and/or popular opinion, to realize their objectives.

Rida refrained from direct involvement in politics throughout Abduh's life. The various political events that took place after Abduh's death, i.e. the decline of Ottoman military strength, the outbreak of World War I, the Arab revolt and its aftermath, made the temptation of political involvement simply too strong to resist. Thus, we find him after the C.U.P. coup of 1909, expressing in *Manar* his admiration of the accomplishments of political associations:

> What do I say in regard to the strength of [political] associations? It is they that destroyed the fortresses of injustice and the temples of oppression and liberated nations and people from slavery...[284]

Rida became involved with four political associations: *Jamᶜiyyat al-Shura al-ᶜUthmaniyyah* (The Ottoman Consultative Association), *Hizb al-Lamarkaziyyah al-ᶜUthmani* (The Ottoman Decentralization Party), *Jamᶜiyyat al-Jamiᶜah al-ᶜArabiyyah* (Association of the Arab League), and *Hizb al-Ittihad al-Suri* (Syrian Unity Party).

Jamᶜiyyat al-Shura al-ᶜUthmaniyyah (Ottoman Consultative Association)

From its inception, *Manar* was banned from Ottoman Syria.[285] *Manar* was so treated not because it was hostile to the Ottoman state; indeed, *Manar* frequently spoke highly of Sultan Abd al-Hamid and his policies.[286] The reason lay, rather, in *Manar*'s close identification with al-Afghani and the Islamic reform movement, as was made evident in a letter to Rida from Abu al-Huda al-Sayyadi (Sultan Abd al-Hamid's closest religious confidant). *Manar*, he wrote, was guilty of echoing "the stray ideas of he who was disguised as an Afghan, Jamal al-Din. You have even described him to have been a Husayni [i.e. a descendant of the Prophet], when in fact government records show him to have been an Iranian from among the most debased of the *Shiᶜah*."[287] Abd al-Hamid's government harassed Rida's family in Tripoli because of Rida's refusal to change *Manar*'s reformist course. When Rida's father visited Cairo to try to persuade his son to make peace with al-Sayyadi, Rida wrote al-Sayyadi a letter of reconciliation and asked Abduh to write a similar letter, to which Abduh agreed. Along with his letter, Abduh sent an autographed copy of his *Risalat al-Tawhid* (Treatise on Monotheism).[288] Though al-Sayyadi accepted the gesture and wrote a letter to Abduh, thanking him for his gift, *Manar* remained banned in Ottoman Syria. Approximately two years after Abduh's death, Rida became involved in *Jamᶜiyyat al-Shura al-ᶜUthmaniyyah*. In explaining how this came about, Rida wrote:

> We used to receive some news of [Ottoman] oppression...
> And after the death of the teacher and leader [Abduh],
> we began to spend our leisure time, previously occupied
> by gatherings with him [Abduh], in gatherings with our
> Ottoman brothers who were residing in Cairo. Through
> them, we came to know more about how severe the
> situation was in the empire and how dangerous the
> future seemed. Thus we founded *Jamᶜiyyat al-Shura
> al-ᶜUthmaniyyah* for the purpose of convincing other
> Ottomans of the need to replace the government of
> oppression with a government of mutual consultation
> [i.e. parliamentary representation]. We did so knowing
> that *Jamᶜiyyat al-Ittihad wa-al-Taraqqi* [C.U.P.] was
> comprised of Muslims in particular. Ottomans, however,
> will remain weak and their oppressors will remain strong
> as long as they are disunited...Thus, we founded our
> association from Muslims...and Christians...Further, we
> asked Jews to join...[289]

According to Rida, *Jamᶜiyyat al-Shura al-ᶜUthmaniyyah* had a secret publication which it distributed throughout the empire to advocate its principles.[290] Rida further related that Ahmet Riza (no relation), a representative of the C.U.P.

before it seized power, contacted *Jam^ciyyat al-Shura al-^cUthmaniyyah* while on a visit to Egypt and proposed its merger with the C.U.P.[291] This, however, was refused by the association's founders since they believed that contrary to their association, the C.U.P. was confined in membership to Muslims.[292] Since its primary objective was the restoration of the constitution, *Jam^ciyyat al-Shura al-^cUthmaniyyah* lost its *raison d'etre* after the restoration of the constitution in 1908. As Rida related, the association's demise quickly followed.[293]

Hizb al-Lamarkaziyyah al-^cUthmani (Ottoman Decentralization Party)

After the C.U.P. coup, Rida traveled to Istanbul to examine closely the new political climate and to try to raise funds for the previously noted *Jam^ciyyat al-Da^cwah wa-al-Irshad*. The official response to Rida's fund raising project was highly reflective of the attitude of the new Ottoman leadership. Rida was told the institution must be named *"anjuman ilm va-irshad* [a Turkish translation of the institution's name]", and must be placed under the supervision of the Grand Mufti in Istanbul.[294] The insistence on giving the institution a Turkish name reflected the C.U.P.'s strong Turkish nationalist attitude and the Turkification policy of Enver Pasha, the principal figure in the C.U.P.'s triumvirate. The demand that the association be placed under the supervision of the Grand Mufti, on the other hand, reflected the C.U.P.'s vision of a strong centralized empire.[295] Rida politely refused the conditions and returned to Cairo where he proceeded, not only to found *al-Da^cwah wa-al-Irshad*, but also to participate in the creation of *Hizb al-Lamarkaziyyah al-^cUthmani.*[296]

Hizb al-Lamarkaziyyah al-^cUthmani was an open political association.[297] Its objective was to decentralize the Ottoman empire. Nevertheless, it laid much emphasis on maintaining the territorial integrity of the Ottoman state.[298] This stand appears to have been rooted in the following factors. First, the Ottoman empire, despite its weakened status, still represented to many intellectuals, including Rida, one of the few remaining Muslim states not yet colonized by Europe. Second, members of *Hizb al-Lamarkaziyyah al-^cUthmani* feared that in the event that the Ottoman empire was broken up, its Arab regions would be vulnerable to European colonial ambitions. Finally, members of *Hizb al-Lamarkaziyyah al-^cUthmani* must have also wanted to be cautious regarding how their association would be perceived in Istanbul and, thus, emphasized Ottoman unity and integrity to ensure that the authorities in Istanbul would not consider their association an enemy of the state.

Many of the principal figures who took part in founding *Hizb al-Lamarkaziyyah al-^cUthmani* late in 1912, were previously involved in *Jam^ciyyat al-Shura al-^cUthmaniyyah*.[299] Their decision to establish *Hizb al-Lamarkaziyyah al-^cUthmani* reflected their disillusionment with the C.U.P. and its policies.[300] George Antonius specifies among the founders of *Hizb al-Lamarkaziyyah al-^cUthmani* the following persons: Rafiq Azm, Rashid Rida, Iskandar Ammun, Fuad al-Khatib, Salim Abd al-Hadi, Hafiz al-Said, Naif Tillu, and Ali al-Nashashibi.[301]

Muhammad Izzat Darwazah adds Muhibb al-Din al-Khatib, Shubli Shumayl, Numan Abu Shair, Dawud Barakat, and Sami al-Jaridini. He also informs us of the association's four highest officers: Rafiq Azm, 'president', Iskandar Ammun, 'vice-president', Rafiq Azm, 'secretary', and Fuad Khatib, 'vice-secretary'.[302] It is only Amin Said who identifies Rida as the spokesman of *Hizb al-Lamarkaziyyah al-ᶜUthmani*.[303]

Jamᶜiyyat al-Jamiᶜah al-ᶜArabiyyah (Association of the Arab League)

At the same time that Rida was active in *Hizb al-Lamarkaziyyah al-ᶜUthmani*, he was also involved with *Jamᶜiyyat al-Jamiᶜah al-ᶜArabiyyah*. Almost everything we know about *Jamᶜiyyat al-Jamiᶜah al-ᶜArabiyyah* comes from Amin Said's *al-Thawrah al-ᶜArabiyyah al-Kubra* (The Great Arab Revolt).[304] Darwazah suggests that Said's account of *Jamᶜiyyat al-Jamiᶜah al-ᶜArabiyyah* is based on pamphlets which were secretly circulated in Syria prior to World War I.[305] Since none of these pamphlets are extant, much of Said's account cannot be verified. Nevertheless, Rida's involvement with *Jamᶜiyyat al-Jamiᶜah al-ᶜArabiyyah*, is confirmed by a number of statements made by Rida in *Manar,* more than fifteen years after the association had ceased to exist.[306] Said's short account related that Rida created *Jamᶜiyyat al-Jamiᶜah al-ᶜArabiyyah* around 1912 with the aim of secretly warning Arab leaders of the dangers arising out of the C.U.P.'s nationalist and centralizing policies and the overall weakness of the Ottoman military forces.[307] Rida corresponded with a number of Arab leaders, including al-Imam Yahya Ibn Hamid al-Din of Yemen, al-Imam Abd al-Aziz Ibn Suᶜud of Najd, and Muhammad Ali al-Idrisi of Asir, all of whom are reported by Said to have responded favorably to Rida's ideas.[308] Only one political leader, however, appears to have actually joined *Jamᶜiyyat al-Jamiᶜah al-ᶜArabiyyah*: al-Amir Abd Allah Ibn Husain of Hijaz who subsequently became the first ruler of modern Jordan.[309] According to Said, Rida also propagated the principles of *Jamᶜiyyat al-Jamiᶜah al-ᶜArabiyyah* in the Persian Gulf region on his way back to Egypt from a trip to India which he undertook in 1913.[310] In particular, Rida appears to have contacted Sultan Faisal of Oman, and Mubarak Ibn al-Sabah of Kuwait.[311] Later, while on a pilgrimage to Mecca in 1916, he appears to have distributed a pamphlet containing the principles of *Jamᶜiyyat al-Jamiᶜah al-ᶜArabiyyah*.[312]

Hizb al-Ittihad al-Suri (Syrian Unity Party)

World War I and its aftermath shattered the objectives of *Hizb al-Lamarkaziyyah al-ᶜUthmani* and *Jamᶜiyyat al-Jamiᶜah al-ᶜArabiyyah*. During the initial years of the French and British mandate, however, new political associations emerged, intent on terminating the French mandates imposed on modern Syria and Lebanon and the British mandates over modern Iraq, Jordan and Palestine. Among these associations was *Hizb al-Ittihad al-Suri*, created in Cairo in 1921 by Rida, along with a number of Syrian nationalists.[313] *Hizb al-Ittihad al-Suri* called for the termination of the French mandate over Syria, and the preservation of Syrian administrative unity.[314] Michel Lutf Allah, a Christian from Lebanon, was elected president of *Hizb al-Ittihad al-Suri* and Rida was elected its vice president.[315] The principal activity undertaken by *Hizb al-Ittihad al-Suri* was sponsoring a conference (June 1921) in Geneva known as *al-Mu'tamar al-Suri al-Filastini* (The Syrian Palestinian Congress), in which all political associations created in response to the imposition of mandates over Syria, Lebanon and Palestine participated.[316] On September 21, 1921, the associations represented at the conference issued a statement calling on the League of Nations to:

(1) Recognize the independence and national sovereignty of Syria, Lebanon, and Palestine.
(2) Recognize the right of these countries to unite.
(3) Terminate the mandates immediately.
(4) Order the withdrawal of French and British troops.
(5) Terminate the Balfour Declaration...[317]

With the subsequent solidification of the French mandate and Prince Faisal's expulsion from Syria, however, the activity of *Hizb al-Ittihad al-Suri* ceased.

None of the political associations Rida became involved with were directed against the British occupation of Egypt. In fact, Rida maintained a positive relationship with British officials in Egypt, to the extent of agreeing to provide them with some services. In particular, prior to the inception of World War I, Rida agreed to send emissaries to a number of Arab rulers to determine their position on an anti-Ottoman Arab revolt.[318] Further, at no point did Rida utilize *Manar* to call on Egyptians to actively resist British occupation. Rida seems to have reasoned that he could not afford to risk his base of operation, especially when few other Muslim countries would have allowed him the freedom he enjoyed in Egypt. It was perhaps this political stance of Rida that prompted Muhammad Kurd Ali (d. 1953), a Syrian thinker who is well known for his Arab nationalist ideas, to write: "he [i.e. Rida] was not well grounded nor trained in politics. He was not taught politics, nor did he know how to practice it."[319] While, Kurd Ali could accuse Rida of political naiveté, he could not accuse him of treason. Such an accusation could simply not be reconciled with Rida's overall political record. Rida's involvement with the political associations, noted above, despite their failure to realize their objectives, endowed him with a mantle of credibility which protected him, both in his life and after his death, from being dismissed as an agent of colonialism.

As regards the internal dynamics of political associations, Rida applied a lesson he undoubtedly learned from al-Afghani. He not only agreed to participate with non-Muslims in the creation of political associations as al-Afghani earlier did in Egypt, but, as noted, he even refused to participate in the C.U.P. on grounds that it did not include Christians or Jews. In so doing, Rida was carrying out a basic policy principle of Islamic reform which was to work jointly with non-Muslims towards resisting Western colonialism and authoritarian governments. Granted, *Jamᶜiyyat al-Shura al-ᶜUthmaniyyah, Hizb al-Lamarka-ziyyah al-ᶜUthmani,* and *Hizb al-Ittihad al-Suri* were not the only associations in which Muslims and Christians cooperated. What makes Rida's cooperation with Christians and Jews particularly significant, however, is the fact that he represented Islamic reform, a religious movement which had significant moral authority over its supporters. Rida demonstrated that a strong commitment to Islam is not only compatible with strong Muslim-Christian-Jewish cooperation, but that it was also compatible with Muslim involvement in institutions led by non-Muslims, as was the case in *Hizb al-Ittihad al-Suri*, provided their objectives were the same.

Youth Associations

Rida used political associations to engage in the struggle to reform the Ottoman empire, to create an independent Arab state, and, finally, to terminate the French mandate over Syria. Having been defeated in all three struggles, Rida proceeded to direct the Islamic reform movement in yet another direction: 'cultural resistance' to Western colonialism and authoritarian governments. In the late 1920s, almost every Muslim country was dominated by some type of Western colonialism. While, in some Muslim countries traditional institutions had still enough vigor to inspire an anti-colonial resistance, e.g. *al-Tariqah al-Sanusiyyah* (The Sanusi Order) in Libya, the vast majority of traditional institutions, having fallen under government control, had lost much of their capacity to mobilize the populace. Rida's challenge, hence, was to create an institution that had strong links not to the political elite but, rather, to the common individual.

Jamᶜiyyat al-Shubban al-Muslimin (Young Men's Muslim Association)

Rida understood 'cultural resistance' as the attempt to ensure that the religious and linguistic identity of the Muslim world would survive the experience of Western colonialism. Thus, it is not surprising that the founding of *Jamᶜiyyat al-Shubban al-Masihiyin* (The Young Men's Christian Association) in Cairo, immediately prior to World War I, as well as the intensification of Christian missionary activity in Egypt after the end of the war would alarm him. He wrote in 1927, regarding the desirability of creating a youth association:

> ...my mind was for a long time preoccupied with how Muslims are in need of such an association...I remained for years researching its history and its development...I, then, asked Tawfiq Diyab, the famous orator, during the Great War [World War I] to investigate the matter and find whether we could create an association for Muslims like that of *Jamᶜiyyat al-Shubban al-Masihiyin* [the Association of Christian Youth], which would abide by the

apolitical character associated with such an association, or whether the military authority would object. Then I learned from him and others that it would not be possible to create such an association at that time.[320]

Rida's efforts towards the creation of a youth association were realized in 1927, when the Cairo based *Jamᶜiyyat al-Shubban al-Muslimin* (Association of Muslim Youth) was founded.[321] Rida, who was one of the major founders of *Jamᶜiyyat al-Shubban al-Muslimin*, wrote in *Manar:* "Of all the associations I took part in creating—with the exception of *Jamᶜiyyat al-Daᶜwah wa-al-Irshad*—no association brought me a stronger sense of satisfaction than this did [i.e. *Jamᶜiyyat al-Shubban al-Muslimin*]."[322] In addition to Rida, several religious scholars played a role in the creation of *Jamᶜiyyat al-Shubban al-Muslimin*, including Abd al-Aziz Jawish, Abd al-Hamid Saᶜd, and Muhibb al-Din al-Khatib.[323] A number of Western educated figures joined the association shortly after its creation, including Muhammad Ahmad al-Ghamrawi, who had studied in England, Yahya Ahmad al-Dardiri, who had studied in Switzerland, and Ali Mazhar, who had studied in Austria.[324]

Jamᶜiyyat al-Shubban al-Muslimin declared as its objectives: (i) To teach Islamic morals and ethics; (ii) To disseminate knowledge in a manner that is compatible with the spirit of the age; (iii) To work towards ending dissensions and abuses among Muslim sects and groups; (iv) To make use of the best of what Eastern and Western civilizations have to offer and to reject all that is bad in them.[325] *Jamᶜiyyat al-Shubban al-Muslimin*'s activity fell into two categories. On the one hand, it sponsored lectures by religious scholars from various Muslim countries and also by Western scholars, and published a journal, *al-Nashrah* (The Publication), in which articles by its members and other contributors were published.[326]

On the other hand, in spite of article two of its constitution which affirmed its apolitical character, *Jamᶜiyyat al-Shubban al-Muslimin* sponsored a number of political activities aimed against European colonial practices in the region, and against the activities of Christian missionaries.[327] *Jamᶜiyyat al-Shubban al-Muslimin* sent telegrams to the League of Nations, the British Foreign Office and the High Commissioner in Jerusalem affirming the rights of Palestinians.[328] When news of a 'French plan' to convert the Berbers surfaced, *Jamᶜiyyat al-Shubban al-Muslimin* called on " the Islamic associations throughout the world" to confront French colonial policy in North Africa.[329] *Jamᶜiyyat al-Shubban al-Muslimin* also issued strong letters addressed to the Egyptian Minister of Interior and to *Shaikh al-Azhar*, protesting the activity of Christian missionaries, and it published pamphlets which responded to attacks on Islamic beliefs, allegedly written by Christian missionaries.[330]

The rise of reformist youth associations was not confined to Egypt. In a consistent pattern, supporters of the Islamic reform movement created such institutions in Syria, North Africa, India, and other Muslim countries. In many cases, the founders of these institutions were religious scholars who described themselves as disciples of Abduh or Rida. In 1938, *Jam⁽iyyat al-⁽Ulama'* (Association of Religious Scholars) was founded in Damascus by Muhammad Kamil al-Qassab, a close associate of Rida who had participated in the activity of *Jam⁽iyyat al-Jami⁽ah al-⁽Arabiyyah* (the Association of the Arab League).[331] Like *Jam⁽iyyat al-Shubban al-Muslimin*, *Jam⁽iyyat al-⁽Ulama'* described itself as an apolitical institution, and, like *Jam⁽iyyat al-Shubban al-Muslimin*, it too was deeply involved in politics. Perhaps the most important political stance taken by *Jam⁽iyyat al-⁽Ulama'* was its strong warning to the government of Prime Minister Jamil Mardam not to sign the *Qanun al-Tawa'if* (Law of Religious Sects) proposed by the French, which gave religious minorities equal status with the *Sunni* Muslim majority. Though Mardam did sign the law, the subsequent public outcry which *Jam⁽iyyat al-⁽Ulama'* helped to fuel, forced him to resign.[332]

In 1931, *Jam⁽iyyat al-⁽Ulama' al-Muslimin* (Association of Muslim Religious Scholars) was founded in Algeria by Ibn Badis (d. 1940), considered to be the founder of the Algerian Islamic reform movement. *Jam⁽iyyat al-Shubban al-Muslimin* (Association of Muslim Youth) was also founded in 1935 in Tunisia by Muhammad al-Tahir Ibn Ashur (d. 1973), destined to become one of the major figures of the Tunisian Islamic reform movement.[333] Both Ibn Badis and Ibn Ashur were strong supporters of Rida and, like him, identified themselves as disciples of Abduh.[334] A similar institution, *Jam⁽iyyat al-⁽Ulama' bi-al-Hind* (The Association of Religious Scholars in India) was created at an even earlier date than Egypt's *Jam⁽iyyat al-Shubban al-Muslimin* (1919).[335] Among those who participated in its creation were members of the aforementioned benevolent association, *Nadwat al-⁽Ulama'*.

After World War I, the Islamic reform movement sought to break away from the elitism which had characterized its earlier benevolent and political associations. While in 1899, an article in *Manar* regarding the sponsorship of associations stated: "Such institutions require conditions which cannot be fulfilled except by the Muslim community's notables and great figures", twenty eight years later, an article in *Manar* described university students as "the most qualified for undertaking its [the youth association's] creation."[336] The activities of reformist youth associations were highly successful in attracting the attention of educated Muslim youth.[337] Once involved, however, their activity was not confined to the literary realm. As previously noted, members of youth associations engaged in very political actions.

The primary significance of youth associations lies not so much in what they achieved in themselves, but, rather, in what they facilitated, that is, the rise of the political parties of Islamic reform. In Egypt, as attested by Hasan al-Banna, the rise of *Ikhwan* was significantly facilitated by *Jam⁽iyyat al-Shubban al-Muslimin*.[338] Johannes Reissner in *Muslimbruder*, has shown how benevolent and youth associations created by Syrian supporters of Islamic reform in the first third of the twentieth century, served as the prototype for the subsequent rise of the Syrian branch of *Ikhwan* (1944).[339] Further, Abu al-Ala al-Mawdudi, the creator of *Jama'at-i Islami* (The Islamic Group) of India, and subsequently of Pakistan, was the editor-in-chief of the publication issued by *Jam'iyyat al-'Ulama' bi al-Hind*, the youth association noted above.[340]

Al-Ikhwan al-Muslimun (The Muslim Brotherhood) – Association Stage

Hasan al-Banna, the founder of *al-Ikhwan al-Muslimun*, was born in 1906 in the Egyptian village of al-Mahmudiyyah into a religious family.[341] Al-Banna encountered members of *al-Tariqah al-Hisafiyyah* (The Hisafi Order) at the young age of twelve and was initiated into the order by Abd al-Wahhab al-Hisafi, the order's Master, at the age of sixteen.[342] It is indeed significant that in addressing his involvement with *al-Tariqah al-Hisafiyyah*, al-Banna empha-sized that his attraction to the institution was based not only on his thirst for a spiritual experience, but also on his admiration of its founder's "firm commit-ment to demanding that which is good and forbidding what is immoral," even when the application of this commitment involved confronting the power of the state.[343] To further illustrate this distinct characteristic of the order's founder, al-Banna related a number of examples, including the following:

> And he [Abd al-Wahhab], along with a number of other religious scholars entered into a gathering attended by Khedive Tawfiq. He offered his greeting in a loud voice. The Khedive, however, answered only with a signal from his hand. So he stated strongly and firmly: "The reply to a greeting is to be made either with a greeting identical to it or by one better than it. Thus, you should say: 'And on you be God's peace and blessings.' It is not proper to respond by a mere hand gesture." The Khedive had no alternative but to comply and praise the Master's words as a testimony to his religious commitment.[344]

The accounts related by al-Banna, irrespective of their historical accuracy, reflect *al-Tariqah al-Hisafiyyah*'s inclination towards 'moral activism', that is, manifesting one's spirituality through community reform, rather than through meditation and prayers alone.

A certain Mrs. White, president of a Christian missionary association, was very active in al-Banna's village.[345] As was the case with many other Muslim reformers, al-Banna seems to have admired Mrs. White for her religious dedi-cation, exhibited by her willingness to live in the very difficult conditions of rural Egypt, though his admiration was more implicit than explicit.[346] What al-Banna was very definite about was his sense of alarm and strong desire to protect the Islamicity of his village from the Christian mission.[347] The mission of Mrs. White was the primary inspiration for al-Banna's creation, in 1922, of *al-Jam'iyyah al-Hisafiyyah al-Khayriyyah* (The Hisafi Benevolent Association). The association, which was located in al-Mahmudiyyah, is described by al-Banna as a "*jam'iyyah islahiyyah* [reformist association]"[348] The primary objective of the association, in addition to the propagation of Islamic morals, was "confronting the activities of the Evangelical missions [of Christians, or specifically Mrs. White]."[349]

Much has been said on the impact of the West on the intellectual development of Islamic reform.[350] *Al-Jam'iyyah al-Hisafiyyah al-Khayriyyah* exhibits some of the institutional influences of the West on the Islamic reform movement. Al-Banna perceived *al-Tariqah al-Hisafiyyah* as inadequately prepared to confront the Christian mission which had arrived in his village. Thus, he decided to rise to the challenge and confront the 'Western transplant' on its own terms. He organized his fellow members of *al-Tariqah al-Hisafiyyah* into an association, an institution which was not bound by the spiritual order's focus on moral training. Al-Banna does not elaborate on the activities carried out by *al-Jam'iyyah al-Hisafiyyah al-Khayriyyah*, nor about the extent to which it was successful in 'protecting' his village from the Christian mission. Nevertheless, his account of its creation remains significant in that it documents his early involvement with Western institutions.

Al-Banna was one of the many Muslims attracted to *Manar*. He writes in his memoirs that he was a frequent reader of *Manar at* the age of sixteen, and that after migrating to Cairo he often visited gatherings in which Rida was the primary speaker.[351] Commenting on Rida's death in 1935, al-Banna wrote in his memoirs:

> On the evening of Thursday, Jamada al-'Ula 23, 1354, which corresponds to August 22, 1935, al-Sayyid Muhammad Rashid Rida, founder of the Islamic *Manar* died, after it had entered into its thirty fifth year. Two editions of its thirty fifth volume were published. Its publication thus terminated after it had functioned throughout this period as a school which inspired many of the representatives of the contemporary Islamic revival.[352]

The termination of *Manar*'s publication was so disturbing to al-Banna that he even sought permission from Rida's family to allow *Ikhwan* to take over the journal.[353] Though he succeeded in acquiring their permission and proceeded to publish a number of issues under the sponsorship of *Ikhwan*, *Manar*'s license was canceled by the government of Husain Sirri Pasha on July 18, 1939, bringing to a halt al-Banna's attempt to perpetuate its publication.[354] After completing his preparatory schooling in Damanhur's Junior Teachers' School, al-Banna migrated along with his family to Cairo and enrolled in *Dar al-'Ulum* (now part of the University of Cairo). Al-Banna graduated in 1927 and was subsequently appointed as a government school teacher in the canal town of al-Ismailiyyah. In his memoirs, al-Banna recollected that shortly after he was stationed in al-Ismailiyyah, *Jam'iyyat al-Shubban al-Muslimin* was created.[355] Since the association was tied to many figures whom al-Banna had come to know and respect during his studies at Cairo, i.e. Rida, Muhibb al-Din al-Khatib, and Abd al-Hamid Sa'd, he received the news of its creation with much enthusiasm.[356] Al-Banna further informs us that he became a member of *Jam'iyyat al-Shubban al-Muslimin* and gave a lecture at its center while on a visit to Cairo.[357]

Ikhwan was founded by al-Banna in March 1928.[358] His decision to create *Ikhwan* so shortly after the inception of *Jam'iyyat al-Shubban al-Muslimin*, appears to have been based on his perception that *Jam'iyyat al-Shubban al-Muslimin* was overly involved in intellectual activity and, more importantly, as generally distant from the popular segment of the community.[359] Al-Banna writes in *Mudhakkarat* that he decided against creating a spiritual order, because (a) he did not want to be perceived by other spiritual orders active in al-Ismailiyyah as trying to compete with them, and (b) he did not want to become involved in an institution devoted primarily to moral training.[360] Al-Banna's choice of the association, rather than the spiritual order, as the institutional structure of *Ikhwan*, however, did not protect him from the hostility of spiritual orders. Immediately after he created *Ikhwan*, al-Banna was ousted from the Hisafi order.[361] Abd al-Wahhab al-Hisafi, the order's Master, viewed al-Banna's creation of *Ikhwan* as incompatible with his membership in the Hisafi order.[362] Indeed, given the intense political activities in which *Ikhwan* was destined to become involved during the 1940s, al-Hisafi's stand was not all together inaccurate, at least not in the long run.

Omar Imady

Chapter 5

Political Parties

In 1933, after five years of organizing *Ikhwan* in al-Ismailiyyah and its neighboring villages, al-Banna was transferred by the Ministry of Education to Cairo.[363] Cairo of the 1930s was a highly politicized city. As previously noted, a parliament had been established in Egypt in 1923. *Hizb al-Wafd* (The Delegation party) was the only political party which had wide popular support. It was led by Sa'd Zaghlul until his death in 1927 and later by Mustafa al-Nahas Pasha. Other important parties, though generally limited in membership to small influential groups, were *al-Hizb al-Watani* (The National Party), *Hizb al-Ahrar al-Dusturiyyin* (The Liberal Constitutional Party), and *Hizb al-Sha'b* (The People's Party), and *Hizb al-Ittihad* (The Union Party).[364]

Undermining Egypt's parliamentary system was the fact that the constitution granted the King the right to appoint prime ministers who were not members of the majority party in parliament. Hence, success in parliament did not necessarily translate into control of the government. The King, rather, appointed a prime minister from one of the minority parties which generally supported his interests. Because of this situation, one of the most important concerns of Egyptians during the 1920s and 1930s, i.e. the presence of British forces in Egypt, could not be satisfactorily addressed. While the attempt of a minority-led government to negotiate a treaty with the British was undermined by *al-Wafd*, the attempt of a majority-led government to negotiate a treaty was undermined by the King.

In 1930, a minority government led by Ismail Sidqi suspended the 1923 constitution. Until 1936, *al-Wafd* boycotted elections and channeled popular frustration, which was at its height, into large demonstrations and strikes. Finally in 1936, elections on the basis of the 1923 constitution were held and *al-Wafd* won a large majority. King Fuad appointed al-Nahas Pasha, *al-Wafd*'s leader, Prime Minister. He began at once to negotiate a treaty with England intended to result in the evacuation of its forces from Egypt. A treaty agreement was indeed reached, though it fell short of fully satisfying nationalist aspirations. Egypt was recognized as an independent sovereign state, but 10,000 British forces were allowed to be stationed in the Canal Zone. Roads and barracks built for these troops were to be financed by Egypt, and, in wartime, all restrictions on the British military presence were to be suspended. Further, the treaty left the question of Sudan's relationship with Egypt unresolved.[365]

Al-Wafd continued to enjoy wide support after the 1936 treaty. Nevertheless, the continuing presence of British forces, mounting agricultural and economic problems, and, later, Zionist activity in Palestine, all served to create a vacuum of moral leadership which various political parties competed to fill. By all accounts, it was *Ikhwan* that best succeeded in achieving this goal.

Al-Ikhwan al-Muslimun (The Muslim Brotherhood) – Political Party Stage

Al-Banna's strong positions on the necessity of total British withdrawal from Egypt, and on aiding Arabs in Palestine (at a time when most Egyptian politicians paid no attention to events in other Arab countries) explain why large segments of the nationalist movement were attracted to *Ikhwan* throughout the 1930s and the 1940s. Further, al-Banna, as attested by friend and foe alike, was very eloquent, capable of conveying his views with both clarity and a deep sense of sincerity. In a speech delivered in Alexandria, al-Banna summarized the vision of *Ikhwan*, as follows:

> Now, I can see within you the legacy of our great Prophet. I would like to know to what extent Alexandria is ready to protect this legacy before I begin to describe its major components [loud cries can be heard promising to protect the legacy]...this legacy can be summarized in three major concepts: 'a model to emulate', 'a mission', and 'a state'. As for the model to emulate, it is the perfect physical and moral characteristics of the Messenger of God...As for the mission, it can be described in three words: faith, a loving upright life, and brotherhood...And as for the state, it rests on three cornerstones: justice, freedom, and struggle...[366]

Al-Banna's vision of a state which reflected Islamic values constituted an operational version of the 'political principle' of Islamic reform. While Abduh was concerned with identifying the character of an Islamic government, al-Banna was concerned with creating it:

> It may be permissible for Muslim reformers to be satisfied with preaching and guiding if it were the case that those in charge listened to God's commandments and obeyed

> them...With the situation as it is now—that is, Islamic
> law is in one valley and actual legislation is in another—
> it is a severe crime for Muslim reformers to shy away
> from seeking to govern...[367]

Al-Banna presented the necessity of creating an Islamic state as being to-
tally harmonious with the reformist principles articulated by Abduh and Rida.
In an editorial published in *al-Nadhir* (The Warner) in 1938, al-Banna wrote:

> Islam is worship and leadership, a religion and a state;
> spirituality and action; prayer and struggle; obedience
> and governing; a Qur'an and a sword; all of these are
> inseparable from one another...[368]

By 1936, *Ikhwan* synthesized the benevolent/youth associations. While the
'benevolent' component was manifested by the creation of schools for both children and illiterate adults, as well as medical clinics, and mosques, the 'youth'
component was manifested in the sponsorship of lectures, letters protesting the
activity of Christian missionaries and colonial policies, and the publication of
various journals and newspapers, e.g. *Risalat al-Murshid al-ʿAmm* (The Message of the General Guide), *Majallat al-Ikhwan al-Muslimin al-Usbuʿiyyah*
(The Muslim Brotherhood Weekly Journal), and *Majallat al-Nadhir* (Journal of
the Warner).[369] Further, *Ikhwan* had a clear popular dimension manifested in the
significant number of workers, small scale merchants and artisans which it succeeded in attracting.[370] In its Fifth General Conference, held in 1939, *Ikhwan*
was described by al-Banna, among other attributes, as a *"hay'ah siyasiyyah*
[political institution]," signifying the willingness of *Ikhwan* to participate in
parliamentary elections.[371]

The outbreak of World War II shortly after this conference, however, created a tense political environment in which many regulations against political activity were imposed by the government. Thus, throughout the war years
Ikhwan was provided with only two opportunities to participate in parliamentary elections. The first opportunity came in February 1942, when al-Nahas
Pasha, who was asked by the King to form a new government, dissolved the
parliament and called for new elections. Al-Banna announced that he would
run as a candidate for al-Ismailiyyah's district.[372] Al-Nahas, however, fearing
that al-Banna's nomination would alarm the British authorities, asked al-Banna
to withdraw.[373] Al-Banna agreed, providing that *Ikhwan* would be allowed to
resume its full activities (which had been suspended by the previous government after the outbreak of World War II) and that the government would take
action against prostitution and the sale of alcoholic beverages.[374] Shortly after
al-Banna's withdrawal, *Ikhwan* was allowed to resume some of its operations,
and restrictions on the sale of alcoholic beverages as well as the closing down
of a number of brothels took place.

The second opportunity came in October, 1944 after a new government was formed by Ahmad Mahir Pasha, leader of the Saᶜdi Party. When preparations began for new parliamentary elections, to be held in January 1945, al-Banna and some of the leading figures of *Ikhwan* announced their candidacies.[375] All of the candidates of *Ikhwan*, however, were defeated.[376] Many observers agreed that the defeat of *Ikhwan*'s candidates was engineered by extensive government distortions of the election results; it was the last time until 1984 that *Ikhwan* would participate in parliamentary elections.[377]

Ironically, al-Banna never spoke of *Ikhwan* as a political party. In fact, he emphatically denied that *Ikhwan* had anything to do with such an institution: "*al-Ikhwan al-Muslimun* is not one of the political parties."[378] During the very period he was leading *Ikhwan* into full participation in parliamentary elections he called for the elimination of all political parties.[379] Al-Banna, rather, preferred to identify *Ikhwan* in terms of abstract concepts: "a new spirit spreading in the heart of this Muslim Nation," "an Islamic Muhammadan message," "a path based on the Prophetic tradition" and " a mystic truth."[380]

Al-Banna's peculiar characterizations of *Ikhwan* are better understood when placed in the context of how political parties were increasingly perceived in Egypt, especially after the 1936 treaty. As noted, the failure of *al-Wafd* to deliver the complete withdrawal of British forces, together with the identification of the vast majority of political parties with corruption and/or loyalty to the King, made the 'political party' a highly discredited institution. Al-Banna, thus, aimed at presenting *Ikhwan* as an attractive 'clean' institutional alternative to the political party which was ready to embrace persons who were disillusioned but still supporters of other political parties. The success of al-Banna's strategy was confirmed by the fact that until the late 1930s, members of *al-Wafd* did not regard it as politically inconsistent to be members of *Ikhwan* as well.[381]

To some members of *Ikhwan*, however, it was both amply clear and highly disturbing that their institution was sponsoring activities that were not consistent with its declared moral character. This is documented by various accounts, including one related by al-Banna himself. He wrote in *Mudhakkarat*:

> Ali Mahir Pasha [Egypt's Prime Minister at the time] attended, along with Abd al-Rahman Azzam Pasha [Head of the Arab League], the Conference on Palestine in London...And after he [Ali Mahir] returned to Egypt, a delegation from among the brothers [i.e. *Ikhwan*], headed by Ahmad al-Sukkari [the Secretary General] went to the train station to receive him. So he [al-Sukkari] called out: Long live Ali Mahir and ordered the brothers to do so also. So some did and some refrained and returned very angry. They sent to me a strong letter of protest in which they mentioned that the brothers are not of those who call

out in praise of people and that they will not do so, but, rather, they will praise God alone...[382]

The members responsible for the letter of protest which al-Banna received were clearly among those who had joined *Ikhwan* because they did not consider it to be a political party and because they believed involvement with political parties to be synonymous with moral contamination. Yet, to the vast majority of members of *Ikhwan*, it was what al-Banna said, rather than what their institution did, that was to be taken seriously. So seriously was *Ikhwan*'s concern with moral authority taken by its members, that one finds them debating very peculiar questions, such as: "Are the brothers [i.e. members of *Ikhwan*] the entire Global Community of Muslims [which would make membership of *Ikhwan* synonymous with being a Muslim], or a community among the Muslims?"[383]

Although Rida frequently attacked the practices of spiritual orders, *Manar* was foremost opposed by *al-Azhar*. This, as earlier explained, was due to the fact that *Manar* usurped *al-Azhar*'s authority. Likewise, it is not surprising that spiritual orders would strongly oppose *Ikhwan*. Indeed, *Ikhwan* was the first institution in Egypt to challenge the spiritual orders' monopoly over recruiting the popular segments of the community to an institution which claimed moral authority. The hostility between *Ikhwan* and the spiritual orders reached its height in 1953, four years after al-Banna's death. Al-Banna's successor, Hasan al-Hudaybi, declared his support for a government proposal to ban spiritual orders in Egypt.[384] Ironically, it was *Ikhwan* which would eventually be banned by Abd al-Nasir, and the spiritual orders which would become the object of government affection and assistance.[385] Government favors, however, are not without price and, in this case, it was providing moral legitimacy for the 1954 crackdown on *Ikhwan*. The orders lived up to Nasir's expectations, branding *Ikhwan* a modern manifestation of *al-Khawarij* [a heretical Muslim sect known for its militant character] and expressing their "disgust" with its "criminal acts."[386]

Chapter 6

Paramilitary Forces

The rise of paramilitary forces in Egypt was clearly inspired by European Fascist models. This is true of *al-Qumsan al-Khudr* (The Green Shirts), founded in 1933 by Ahmad Husain, the leader of *Misr al-Fatat* (Young Egypt), *al-Qumsan al-Zurq* (The Blue Shirts), founded in 1935 by Muhammad Bilal, a member of *al-Wafd*, and *al-Jawwalah* (Rover Troops), founded in 1935 by Hasan al-Banna.[387] However, while paramilitary forces owed their inspiration to European models, they owed their creation to Egypt's charged political climate in the 1930s:

> It was not perhaps mere coincidence that the first appearance of paramilitary groups—the *Wafd*'s 'Blue Shirts' and the 'Green Shirts' of *Misr al-Fatat*—coincided with extra legal manipulation of the constitutional processes by the palace in the early 1930s.[388]

Al-Ikhwan al-Muslimun (The Muslim Brotherhood) – Paramilitary Force Stage

Al-Banna undoubtedly shared the frustrations and fears of *al-Wafd* and *Misr al-Fatat*. His creation of *al-Jawwalah* was not, however, merely motivated by his concern with *Ikhwan*'s security. Al-Banna, rather, perceived *al-Jawwalah* as an instrument through which the '*jihad* principle' of Islamic reform could be implemented. In Islamic history, *jihad* was understood in various ways, including a spiritual struggle against one's desires, a social struggle against ignorance and a military struggle against Islam's enemies.[389] As the activities of *al-Jawwalah* vividly illustrated, al-Banna's conception of *jihad* was at once spiritual, social and militaristic. During its first ten years, *al-Jawwalah* sponsored athletic exercises and scouting activities, i.e. hiking and camping, community services, e.g. aiding the government in its battle against malaria, and various security measures, such as the maintenance of order during demonstrations sponsored by *Ikhwan*.[390] The British military presence in Egypt and the rising hostilities between the Zionists and Arabs in Palestine in the 1940s, however, shifed al-Banna's conception of *jihad* towards the militaristic dimension. Al-Banna writes:

> Allah has obligated *jihad* on every Muslim; a firm and binding obligation from which there is no swaying nor escaping...[391]

> Every land in which the statement 'There is no god but the One God and Muhammad is His Messenger' is proclaimed is part of our land: it has its sanctity and holiness and is entitled to our sincerity and to our *jihad*...[392]

> ...the Muslim community which...is aware of what constitutes a dignified death, is endowed by God with a dignified life...[393]

Although al-Banna's emphasis on armed resistance to Western colonialism appears to contradict Abduh's and Rida's emphasis on 'cultural resistance', in actuality it does not. It was the realization that Muslims were not prepared to resist the West militarily that had prompted Abduh and Rida to commit themselves to 'cultural resistance', that is, 'cultural resistance' was a policy of pragmatism, and not of ideology. Rida, after all, encouraged military resistance against the French in North Africa. Such positions, however, are not to be confused with an endorsement of indiscriminate violence. Nothing in the documented legacy of al-Afghani, Abduh or Rida implies they would have approved of such behavior. Likewise, al-Banna was also strongly against the use of indiscriminate violence to advance political objectives: "Criminal violence can never be accepted as an instrument of attaining freedom."[394] Yet, as documented below, the "criminal violence" that eventually emerged was directly linked to some of the institutional choices which were made by al-Banna.

Late in 1942, al-Banna created *al-Jihaz al-Khass* (The Special Unit) as a secret branch of *al-Jawwalah*.[395] Important differences existed between *al-Jawwalah* and *al-Jihaz al-Khass*. While the former was an open association which sponsored athletic activity and community services, the latter was secret and focused on violent actions. In spite of these differences, however, it was *al-Jawwalah* that provided *al-Jihaz al-Khass* with its members. In their confessions to the government, many of *al-Jawwalah*'s members acknowledged that their induction into *al-Jihaz al-Khass* was treated by their superiors as normal procedure.[396] In a sense, the athletic activity of *al-Jawwalah* had an influence similar to the literary activity of *Jam'iyyat al-Shubban al-Muslimin*, namely attracting individuals who would otherwise refrain from belonging to a reformist institution. Once attracted, it was highly likely that a member of *al-Jawwalah* would eventually find himself part of a group attacking a British establishment in the Suez Canal, fighting in a battalion in Palestine, or even carrying out acts of violence against members of his own community. Thus, despite the non violent activity sponsored by *al-Jawwalah*, its subordination to *al-Jihaz al-Khass* allows for describing both institutions as constituting one cohesive paramilitary force.

The initial task of *al-Jihaz al-Khass* was to train selected members of *al-Jawwalah* in military missions. By the end of World War II, the troops trained by *al-Jihaz al-Khass* were ready for their first mission, attacking the British presence in the Suez Canal.[397] In 1946 and much of 1947, *Ikhwan* undertook a significant number of attacks on British military establishments in the Canal Zone.[398] Though, little is known about the details of these attacks, it is clear that they at times caused damage to property and injury to British personnel.[399] The U.N. resolution dividing Palestine into an Arab and Israeli state in November 1947, however, shifted al-Banna's focus away from the Suez Canal. Al-Banna spoke very strongly in favor of aiding Arabs in Palestine. In a letter addressed to Prime Minister Ali Mahir Pasha, al-Banna once wrote: "The trials, aspirations, and rights of Palestine, Your Excellency, will not be forgotten by Muslims in Egypt and elsewhere."[400] The first documented high level contact between *Ikhwan* and Arabs in Palestine took place in 1935, when al-Banna's brother, Abd al-Rahman, visited Jerusalem and met its Grand Mufti, Amin al-Husayni.[401] In 1936, *Ikhwan* took part in collecting funds to assist the Arab strike in Palestine and carried out an extensive propaganda campaign in support of the demands of the organizers of the strike.[402] In 1944, *Ikhwan* also played an active role in pressuring the government to grant political asylum for Amin al-Husayni who had been deported by British authorities.[403]

None of these actions, however, came close in magnitude to what *Ikhwan* would begin to sponsor in 1947. The head of the Arab League, Abd al-Rahman Azzam Pasha, was a personal friend of al-Banna. Al-Banna used this relationship to work out an agreement with al-Nuqrashi Pasha, Egypt's Prime Minister at the time, which allowed *Ikhwan* to collect funds, purchase weapons and train volunteers, for the purpose of creating *kata'ib* (battalions) to fight against the Zionists in Palestine.[404] Nuqrashi's only condition was that army officers would be responsible for the training of volunteers.[405] Late in 1947, *Ikhwan* had created its first battalion, comprised of 10,000 fighters, most of whom were members of *al-Jawwalah*.[406] Before the war officially began, the battalion had already been stationed in al-Arish.[407] Egyptian army officers would later recollect that members of *Ikhwan* played an admirable role in the war, and that they were particularly helpful in assisting Egyptian soldiers (including Abd al-Nasir) who were besieged in the Falujah pocket in the Gaza Strip by the Israeli army.[408]

Even before the war in Palestine had ended, *al-Jihaz al-Khass* began to carry out acts against Egyptians that had little to do with al-Banna's conception of *jihad* and much to do with terrorism. It was not accidental that the move towards terrorism by *al-Jihaz al-Khass* coincided with a change in its leadership. The change was necessitated by al-Banna's decision, in November 27, 1947, to dismiss Ahmad al-Sukkari, the Secretary General of *Ikhwan*.[409] Salih Ashmawi, the figure al-Banna had previously charged with the creation of *al-Jihaz al-Khass* was appointed the new Secretary General of *Ikhwan* and Abd al-Rahman al-Sandi (who had been active in *al-Jihaz al-Khass* ever since its inception in 1942) was made its new leader.

Al-Sandi was destined to acquire a very peculiar reputation in the historical account of *Ikhwan*, namely, that of being the figure responsible for confusing and then severing the lines of communication between *al-Jihaz al-Khass* and al-Banna; inhibiting, and eventually terminating, al-Banna's ability to control its activity. Al-Sandi's responsibility for the course which *al-Jihaz al-Khass* began to pursue in 1948 is attested to not only by the events that followed his appointment, related below, but also by the fact that *Ikhwan* was consistently cleared of involvement from the many acts of violence that occurred in Cairo prior to his appointment as leader of *al-Jihaz al-Khass*, e.g. the bombing attack on a cinema in May 1946, and the bombing attack on a cinema in May 1947, both of which were undertaken by *Rabitat al-Shabab* (The Association of Youth), a terrorist association founded by members of *al-Wafd*.[410]

On March 22, 1948, an Egyptian judge, Ahmad al-Khazindar, was assassinated while on his way to work by two young men who later confessed to being members of *al-Jihaz al-Khass*.[411] The assassination was undertaken because the judge had ordered the imprisonment of a man who had attacked a British establishment.[412] According to many reports, al-Banna was extremely disturbed by the assassination.[413] Throughout July, August and September, 1948, the Jewish community of Cairo was victim to a host of attacks which not only caused physical damage to property but which were also responsible for many deaths and injuries as well.[414] The role of *al-Jihaz al-Khass* in these acts was discovered after a significant number of documents relating to the activity of *al-Jihaz al-Khass* were seized by mere chance in November 1947.[415] The documents identified the names of some important members who were all promptly arrested.[416]

On December, 8, 1948, the government announced its decision to dissolve *Ikhwan* and confiscate its wealth and property.[417] The decision was presented as a response to a plan by *Ikhwan* to overthrow the government which had manifested itself in a significant number of violent acts undertaken by *Ikhwan* over the previous three years.[418] After the decision was made public, over 4000 members of *Ikhwan* were arrested.[419] Al-Banna was the only leading figure of *Ikhwan* who was spared arrest; an act which he predicted was a prelude to his assassination.[420]

Following the dissolution of *Ikhwan*, al-Banna is reported to have made many attempts to strike a deal with the government which would allow at least some members of *Ikhwan* to be set free; he was, however, consistently turned down by the Prime Minister, al-Nuqrashi Pasha.[421] Only twenty days after al-Nuqrashi ordered the dissolution of *Ikhwan*, he was assassinated by a young man who later acknowledged that he was a member of *al-Jihaz al-Khass*.[422] A new government was formed by a close friend of al-Nuqrashi, Ibrahim Abd al-Hadi.[423] Al-Banna still tried, however, to make peace with the government. Early in 1949, al-Banna wrote a pamphlet entitled *Bayan Li-al-Nas* (A Proclamation for the People) in which he strongly condemned the assassination of al-Nuqrashi.[424] So disturbed was al-Banna by the actions of *al-Jihaz al-Khass* that he is even reported to have acknowledged the necessity of the dissolution of *Ikhwan*, or, according to another account, to have at least regretted its involvement in politics.[425] Yet, the violence of *al-Jihaz al-Khass* continued. After a failed attempt by one of its members to bomb the courthouse in which important documents relating to *al-Jihaz al-Khass* were stored, al-Banna wrote in a public letter to the Ministry of Interior in regard to the culprits: "They are neither brothers nor Muslims."[426] On February 12, 1949, al-Banna himself was assassinated; numerous investigations confirmed that the assassins were agents of Abd al-Hadi's government.[427]

It is hardly an exaggeration to affirm that no institution was more damaging to the Islamic reform movement than that of the paramilitary force. Its role in the events of 1949 was subsequently repeated in 1954, and in 1966. In 1954, despite all the attempts carried out by al-Hudaybi, al-Banna's successor, to terminate the existence of *al-Jihaz al-Khass* and his strong prohibition of the use of violence against Abd al-Nasir's government, members of *al-Jihaz al-Khass* carried out the famous assassination attempt against Abd al-Nasir which was followed by the second dissolution of *Ikhwan* and the execution of six of its members.[428] In 1966, it was members of *al-Jihaz al-Khass* who involved Sayyid Qutb, one of the leading theotricians of *Ikhwan* in the 1960's, in a plot to overthrow the government, despite Qutb's strong rejection of the idea and the violence it entailed.[429] Qutb and two other members of *Ikhwan* were executed in 1966 following the discovery of the plot.

In their totality, these actions, replicated by similar organizations in other Muslim countries, unleashed the full power of the state, invariably supported by Western powers, against the civil institutional layer so carefully nourished by al-Afghani, Abduh, Rida and al-Banna over a period of seventy eight years (1871-1949). This was carried out despite the fact that the vast majority of the components of this institutional layer strongly condemned political and indiscriminate violence. Ironically, what followed was not only the fall of Muslim civil society, but also the rise of a climate that was, and so remains, highly conducive to the growth of organizations that far transcend the militant nature of *al-Jihaz al-Khass* and the violence of its methods. Understanding why the paramilitary force proved to be so utterly damaging to the Islamic reform movement is at the core of the analysis undertaken below.

Part III

The Fall of Muslim Civil Society

Chapter 7

Deconstructing the Fall

Underlying the fall of Muslim civil society were three major forces: (i) the adoption of secular institutional form, (ii) the upholding of moral content, and (iii) government hostility to any form of institutional autonomy.

Adopting Secular Institutional Form

Unlike members of the religious colleges, the spiritual orders and the guilds who belonged to expressive institutions, or institutions that embody a purpose unto themselves, members of *al-Jihaz al-Khass* belonged to an instrumental institution, or an institution that serves as a medium through which a purpose is achieved.[430] It is to be recalled that members of the guilds of merchants and artisans were also members of the spiritual orders. The orders were created to carry out the task of *tarbiyah* (moral training). Such training had a moral value that was autonomous from the political, economic, and social affairs of the community.

It is indeed ironic that no political violence took place in early nineteenth century Cairo, even after Muhammad Ali betrayed the religious scholars and proceeded to destroy the institutional fabric of their community. Without the authorization of the religious scholars, members of the guilds of merchants and artisans would not move against Muhammad Ali, regardless of how powerful and trained they felt after helping force Napoleon's soldiers to withdrawal. They were simply not willing to incur the price of rejecting the authority of the Masters of spiritual orders. Indeed the non secular structure of the guilds and spiritual orders was such that the leader could not be alienated without the total destruction of the power structure. Not so with *Ikhwan*. Members of *al-Jihaz al-Khass* could afford what members of the guilds could not because, contrary to the 'moral' character of the spiritual order, the secular character of the association/political party allowed for the depersonalization of moral authority. To members of the guilds of merchants and artisans, moral authority was embodied in the Master of the order who provided their institution and activities with moral legitimacy, an essential attribute in a community organized on moral grounds. No such obstacles stood in the path of members of *al-Jihaz al-Khass*.

The depersonalization of moral authority was indeed an integral component of the reformist institutional legacy.[431] We have seen how *Manar* was used by Abduh and Rida to teach Qur'anic exegeses, provide legal verdicts, and give moral guidance. In so doing, *Manar* had depersonalized *al-Azhar*'s moral authority. The printed word, rather than the spoken words of the religious scholar, now defined for the Muslim community what constituted orthodoxy. Despite al-Banna's charisma, he did not possess the same moral authority for *Ikhwan* that a Master of a spiritual order did for guild/order members.

At the core of the authority of the Masters of spiritual orders over their disciples was a very intimate and personal relationship. Considering the large number of members of *Ikhwan* (most estimates put the number well over one hundred thousand) it is obvious that many members never even had the chance to meet al-Banna. Granted, they were heavily exposed to his ideas through *Ikhwan*'s publications. Like *Manar*, however, *Ikhwan*'s publications were instruments of depersonalization. Members of the guilds did not read about the ideas of their Master, but, rather, they listened to him speak. As we have seen, al-Banna was highly involved during his youth with spiritual orders. It was those experiences which undoubtedly explain why he consistently expected members of *Ikhwan* to act as if they were members of an expressive institution when in fact they were members of an instrumental institution. An important example of this problem of communication occurred when some members of *Ikhwan* began insisting that al-Banna relinquish some of his administrative authority to facilitate *Ikhwan*'s operation as a political party.[432] Al-Banna responded by forcing the primary spokesman for these members, Ahmad al-Sukkari, the Secretary General of *Ikhwan*, to resign.

Al-Banna did not force al-Sukkari's resignation because he was categorically against engaging *Ikhwan* in political party activity. Indeed, only two years earlier (1945) he had participated in parliamentary elections. Al-Sukkari was ousted because he 'dared' to ask for the distribution of authority in *Ikhwan* to be consistent with its activities. Al-Banna, who at a young age had created *al-Jam°iyyah al-Hisafiyyah,* an 'association of a spiritual order,' wanted both the political viability of the political party and the culture and authority of a spiritual order. The ouster of al-Sukkari, however, did not put an end to the intrinsic instrumental character of *Ikhwan*. It surfaced again in the activities of *al-Jihaz al-Khass* and this time the problem was far more complex than a simple ouster could eliminate.

Not only does the institutional form of *al-Jihaz al-Khass* explain why its members became detached from al-Banna's authority, but it also explains their resilience in the face of numerous government crackdowns from 1948 onwards. Muhammad Ali, as we have seen, confiscated charitable trusts, created the 'Master of all Masters of Spiritual Orders' position, and imposed regulations over the guilds. In so doing, Muhammad Ali only suppressed the 'potential' of these institutions to threaten his authority. He did not suppress their 'purpose'. The religious scholars still taught 'God's law', the Masters of spiritual orders still taught 'God's love' and members of the guilds still manufactured and traded products. The purpose/potential attribute, however, is peculiar to expressive institutions. The government's attempts to suppress the potential of *al-Jihaz al-Khass*, that is, its capacity to carry out acts of violence, was synonymous with the attempt to suppress the purpose of *al-Jihaz al-Khass*, a fact which its members were well aware of. Members of *al-Jihaz al-Khass* believed in political violence and they were determined to carry out such violence against everyone they believed deserved it, including the Muslim judge who imprisoned nationalist fighters, the Prime Minister who banned *Ikhwan*, and the court house which stored evidence against them.

In short, Muslim reformers clearly failed to comprehend the dynamics of the secular institutional form they were adopting. Deprived of the religious college, they adopted the journal, and deprived of the spiritual order, they adopted the association, the political party and, eventually, the paramilitary force. At no point, however, did Muslim reformers seem to have considered the impact of secular institutional forms on the ideas they stood for, and their relationship with the government. Muslim reformers, rather, seem to have viewed institutional form as something structural that could be objectified and as such, a neutral object which could be infused with any content, including the reformist world-view, without consequences.

The Exception of *Shi'i* Islamic Fundamentalism

It must be emphasized that the rise of Islamic fundamentalism in *Shi'i* Muslim countries, Iran in particular, which culminated in the 'Islamic revolution' of 1979 cannot be explained in terms of secular institutional form. Rather, as has been documented by a number of scholars, *Shi'i* fundamentalism is rooted, conceptually, in a highly revered tradition of martyrdom and, institutionally, in a strong religious establishment which, unlike its *Sunni* counterpart, possessed a centralized mode of authority and additional mechanisms of financial autonomy, i.e. the *khums* (the obligation to donate one fifth of a Muslim individual's profits to the religious scholars).[433] Further, although the *Shi'i* doctrine of *imamah* (religious leadership) designates Muhammad Ibn Hasan al-Askari (d. 874) as the last pure and infallible imam, *Shi'i* religious scholars did, nevertheless, enjoy by virtue of this doctrine significant moral authority over the Muslim community.

Al-Afghani, who strongly advocated the utilization of Western institutions during his stay in Egypt was aware of the mobilizing power embodied in the *Shi^ci* religious establishment. He utilized traditional institutions in his campaign against the economic concessions which the Iranian monarch Nasir al-Din Shah (1848-1896) had granted to the British in 1890. In a letter addressed to the *marja^ce mutlaq* (The chief *Shi^ci* jurist) Hajji Mirza Hasan Shirazi, al-Afghani called on him to use his great moral authority to oppose the concession:

> ...You are the head of the community of truth [i.e. the community of religious scholars] and you are the soul that permeates the individual members of the Muslim community. Thus, none carry out a major action without you...all the religious scholars of Iran are waiting for you...to utter one word...[434]

Shirazi did indeed utter the word al-Afghani desired. He declared in a religious legal verdict that until the 1890 concession given to the British for the purchase, sale and export of tobacco was canceled by Nasir al-Din, Muslims are prohibited from smoking tobacco. The extensive observation of Shirazi's religious legal verdict as well as the unrest it generated, prompted Nasir al-Din Shah to cancel the concession in 1892.

Not only did the *Shi^ci* religious establishment survive the often oppressive policies of Qajar rulers, but it also succeeded in surviving the far more systematic attempt to undermine its authority by the Pahlavis. Granted, the various Westernizing decrees of Reza Shah (1925-1941) weakened the religious scholars' hold over education and judicial affairs. Nevertheless, the religious scholars largely retained their financial and administrative autonomy and their moral authority over the Muslim community. Reza's son, Muhammad Reza, succeeded through his severe authoritarian policies in destroying many political institutions which opposed him. Like his father, however, he failed to dismantle the religious establishment. In short, while Western institutions played an integral role in the rise of *Sunni* Islamic fundamentalism, it was traditional institutions which constituted the foundations of the *Shi^ci* parallel.

Upholding Moral Content

Despite its importance, the secular mode of authority of the institutions adopted by Muslim reformers does not alone fully explain the actions of members of *al-Jihaz al-Khass*. Equally important is the emphatic insistence by Muslim reformers to uphold the moral content of their institutions. Indeed, it is precisely this dangerous mix, as it were, that continues to enflame and further radicalize Islamic fundamentalism. The message is 'Islam', the epitome of non-secularism, but the method was adopted from the West, the heartland of secularism.

Islam has been interpreted by the vast majority of its *Sunni* religious scholars in such a way as to categorically reject the notion of a secular realm of human conduct. True, *Sunni* religious scholars were willing to tolerate for centuries governments which did not live up to Islamic precepts, yet they were not willing for a moment to endow such governments with moral legitimacy. They branded them, rather, as *khilafat al-taghallub* (governments based on a successful usurpation) and did not confuse them with *khilafat al-imamah* (governments based on moral authority).[435]

There was much that Abduh, Rida, and al-Banna wanted to reform, the legitimization of secularism, however, was not on their agenda. Abduh wrote:

> The various traditions upon which Islamic law is based unanimously agree on the necessity of there being an *Imam* (moral leader) who protects Islamic law and who undertakes its application in the Muslim community.[436]

Commenting on Ali Abd al-Raziq's work *al-Islam wa Usul al-Hukm* (Islam and the Foundations of Government), Rida wrote:

> Islam has no moral leader, nor judicial or political laws. It is purely a spiritual religion like the religion of the Christians...

> This is the summary of the new *bidʿah* [innovation] which has been propagated in Muslim countries by Ali Abd al-Raziq...He claims that this is the position of Islam as he understands it. But how can he explain away the political laws which are contained in the Qur'an and the Prophetic traditions, such as the laws regulating treaties of war?[437]

Addressing members of the Muslim Brotherhood, al-Banna stated:

> We believe that the precepts and teachings of Islam organize people's affairs in this world and the Hereafter; and those who think that Islam's teachings only deal with the realm of spirituality and worship are wrong.[438]

This emphatic rejection of the legitimization of secularism by Muslim reformers would have exerted a far less dangerous impact on secular institutional form had it contained an unequivocal condemnation of the use of violence against people and establishments which are not directly involved,—using the strictest definition of 'directly involved'—in an aggressive military campaign against Muslims. While, as noted above, al-Afghani, Abduh, and Rida never spoke in favor of such violence; and while al-Banna spoke and wrote against indiscriminate violence, none of these Muslim reformers were clear enough or unequivocal enough in regard to this issue. Granted, none could have possibly imagined the types of activities undertaken by fundamentalist groups since the late 1940s and until the present. Nevertheless, even religious scholars who presently identify themselves with the legacy of Islamic reform are yet to arrive at the level of categorical clarity required to offset the dangerous mixture of moral content and secular institutional form.[439]

The State: Perpetuating a Conducive Climate

If there was anything in common among the various governments that ruled Egypt from 1871 until 1949, it was strong hostility toward autonomous institutions, especially institutions sponsored by religious scholars. Such institutions were tolerated by Egypt's governments only when they served the regime's purposes, or when an external power, i.e. the British, prevented their suppression. Given the fact that Muhammad Ali brought under government control the network of traditional institutions after having used it to his own advantage it is not surprising that Muslim reformers could not agree with those Muslim intellectuals who perceived Muhammad Ali as a great leader.

In 1902, Muhammad Abduh wrote an essay in *Manar* entitled "Athar Muhammad ᶜAli fi Misr" (The Legacy of Muhammad Ali in Egypt). The essay begins with strong criticism of the Mamluks. But, unlike other essays which began in the same way and then proceeded to praise Muhammad Ali as a great leader, Abduh attacked Muhammad Ali as follows:

> Some ignorant people are not ashamed of saying that Muhammad Ali made of religion the foundation of the walls of his kingdom. What religion was a foundation for Muhammad Ali's kingdom? The religion of collecting taxes? The religion of the whip? He confiscated the charitable trusts of the mosques and replaced these with what is called *fa'id ruznamah* which amounted to one thousandth of their previous funds. He further took from the charitable trusts of *al-Azhar* that which, if it still possessed today, would amount to no less than half a million Egyptian pounds annually. Muhammad Ali's relationship with religion was strictly confined to co-opting some religious scholars through gifts and invitations that he might later use against other religious scholars.[440]

We have seen how the emergence of Western institutions in Egypt was initially encouraged by Khedive Ismail as part of a strategy to ward off the pressure of European creditors. Ismail's reasoning was that while political journals and associations would show him to be a tolerant and enlightened ruler, they would not be allowed to become a threat to his rule. The subsequent autonomous status acquired by these institutions occurred despite Ismail's strong opposition. In spite of his earlier promises to the contrary, Ismail's successor, Tawfiq, attacked autonomous institutions. Nor was Urabi an exception to the rule. In the short period that he was the *de facto* ruler of Egypt, he clearly showed himself to be hostile to reformist institutions; indeed, he was determined to dismantle them.

Though the British occupation of Egypt brought about the termination of al-Afghani's institutions, it was undoubtedly the British insistence that overt legal procedure be followed that allowed the emergence of reformist institutions and protected them from the government's desire to suppress them. Abduh quickly made use of this advantage, employing his friendship with Cromer as a defense against the efforts of Khedive Tawfiq, and later of Khedive Abbas Hilmi, to abort his various reformist projects. Likewise, the advantage of the British presence was well understood by Rida who also maintained a positive relationship with Cromer and, subsequently, with Cromer's successor, Sir Eldon Gorst.

Furthermore, not only was the British presence the active impulse underlying the creation of Egypt's political parties, but it was also responsible for creating a legal climate without which political parties could not operate. Though the British did at times intervene in the political process, it was the Khedive's government which was primarily responsible for whatever corruption existed in Egypt's political party life.

The 1952 revolution swept away the legal framework which made possible the emergence of autonomous civil institutions, reformists and otherwise. *Ikhwan* was initially spared only because Abd al-Nasir, like Muhammad Ali before him, believed they could help bolster his regime which badly needed public support. Once this was accomplished, *Ikhwan* was brutally disposed of, though only after providing Abd al-Nasir with an excellent excuse, i.e. the assassination attempt against him.

Underlying the intolerance of Egypt's governments towards reformist institutions was a serious misperception of the commitment of religious scholars to their once prominent role in the community. The father of this misperception was Muhammad Ali who believed that in undermining the base of the religious scholars' power, he would effectively remove them from the political scene. Shortly after al-Afghani introduced Egypt's religious scholars to the advantages of various Western institutions, they rebounded and played a highly significant role in the first challenge to government authority since the 1804 revolt against the Ottoman governor, i.e. the Urabi revolt of 1882. When, against all odds, a reformist political party was created, they had been again underestimated, this time by Prime Minister Ahmad Mahir Pasha who, through vote fraud, made sure none of the candidates of *Ikhwan* won in the 1945 parliamentary elections. This, however, only facilitated the rise of violence sponsored by *al-Jihaz al-Khass*. By allowing the rise of civil institutions and inhibiting, in the process, the rise of the political context necessary for the healthy democratic operation of these institutions, the government in Egypt, and in other Muslim countries, contributed to the creation of a climate which encouraged the growth of militancy.

Islamic fundamentalism is indeed an unintended product of a process that was initially concerned with reviving Islamic civilization and resisting Western colonialism through the creation of a Muslim civil society. The process was derailed from its original objective because of a peculiar course of events, traced through the course of this study, for which both Muslim reformers and the government must be held equally responsible.

Notes

Notes to Introduction

1. Major works which employ the term 'Islamic reform' as it is employed by this book are: Charles C. Adams, *Islam and Modernism in Egypt: A Study of the Modern Reform Movement Inaugurated by Muhammad Abduh* (New York, 1968 [first published in 1933]), henceforth *Islam and Modernism;* and H. A. R. Gibb, *Modern Trends in Islam* (Chicago, 1947), henceforth *Modern Trends in Islam.* Recent studies of the late nineteenth/early twentieth century still employ the term. See, for example, David Dean Commins, *Islamic Reform: Politics and Social Change in Late Ottoman Syria* (New York, 1990), henceforth *Islamic Reform.* Note: the term 'Islamic militancy' is more popular among Muslim scholars than the term 'Islamic fundamentalism'. See, for example, Saad Eddin Ibrahim, "Islamic Militancy as a Social Movement: The Case of Two Groups in Egypt" in Ali E. Hillal Dessouki, ed., *Islamic Resurgence in the Arab World* (New York, 1982).

2. See, for example, Gilles Kepel, *Muslim Extremism in Egypt: The Prophet and the Pharaoh,* (Berkeley & Los Angeles, 1984), the preface written by Bernard Lewis in particular, and W. M. Watt, *Islamic Fundamentalism and Modernity,* (London, 1988). Note: reflecting the desire of authors to arrive at simple and convincing explanations, the post 9/11 era is replete with works that present Islam as intrinsically violent and intolerant.

3. A *Sunni* Muslim is one who abides by the authority of one of four guilds/schools of law. Presently, the majority of Muslims are *Sunni*.

4. Ibn Taymiyyah, *Manahij al-Sunnah,* (The Guidelines of the Prophetic Path) (Cairo, n.d.), II, 87, and Ibn Taymiyyah, *al-Siyasah al-Shar‘iyyah fi Islah al-Ra‘i wa-al-Ra‘iyyah,* (The Divine Framework for the Ruler and the Ruled) (Cairo, 1971), 185, respectively.

5. The traditional *Sunni* position on the state and the use of violence is clearly expressed by al-Mawardi (d. 1058) in his *Nasihat al-Muluk* (Advice to Kings), (Baghdad, 1986).

6. Youssef M. Choueiri, *Islamic Fundamentalism,* (London, 1988), 10. See also John L. Esposito, *Islamic Threat, Myth Or Reality?,* (New York, 1992); Dilip Hiro, *Holy Wars, The Rise of Islamic Fundamentalism,* (New York, 1989); Dilip Hiro, *Islamic Fundamentalism,* (London, 1988); and Emmanuel Sivan, *Radical Islam, Medieval Theology and Modern Politics,* (New York, 1985).

7. George Makdisi, *Rise of Colleges* (Edinburgh, 1990), 270-280, henceforth *Rise of Colleges.*

8. A number of essays in David Cowely & Paul Heyer, eds., *Communication in History,* (New York, 1991) provide examples of how the adoption of new techniques of communication by a given society had serious and unanticipated consequences on the society's intellectual and political culture. See in particular, Harold Innis, "Media in Ancient Empires", 29-36; James Burke, "Communication in the Middle Ages", 67-77; and Elizabeth Eisenstein, "The Rise of the Reading Public", 94-102.

Notes to Text

1. Lit. Vicegerent – leader of the Muslim state/community.

2. George Makdisi, *Rise of Humanism,* (Edinburgh, 1990), 2-15, henceforth *Rise of Humanism.*

3. *Rise of Humanism,* 16.

4. Makdisi in *Rise of Humanism,* 16-23, defends the notion of *madhahib* constituting guilds of law. See Louis Massignon, "Sinf", in *The Encyclopedia of Islam,* (Leiden, 1913-1938), henceforth *EI1*; Bernard Lewis, "The Islamic Guilds" in *The Economic History Review,* VIII, No. 1 (November, 1937); Ira M. Lapidus, *Muslim Cities in the later Middle Ages,* (Cambridge, 1967); Gabriel Baer, *Egyptian Guilds in Modern Times,* (Jerusalem, 1964), henceforth *Egyptian Guilds*; and Abd al-Aziz Muhammad al-Shinnawi, *Siwar min Dawr al-Azhar* (Images of the Role of al-Azhar), (Cairo, 1971); all of which confirm the existence of guilds in Islamic history.

5. A general treatment of the *madrasah* is found in J. Pedersen—[G. Makdisi], "Madrasa" in *The Encyclopedia of Islam,* (Leiden, 1954 [New Edition]), V, 1123-1134, henceforth *EI2.*

6. A general treatment of the *tariqah* is found in Louis Massignon, "Tarika" in *EI1.* Information on the early development of the *tariqah* is found in: George Makdisi, "Hanbali School and Sufism" in *Humaniora Islamica,* II (1974), 61-72; *Rise of Humanism,* 183; Ira M. Lapidus, *History of Islamic Societies,* (Cambridge, 1988), 254-258; H.A.R. Gibb and Harold Bowen, *Islamic Society and the West: A Study of the Impact of Western Civilization on Moslem Culture in the Near East, I,* (Islamic Society in the Eighteenth Century), pt. 2 (Oxford, 1962), 75, henceforth *Islamic Society.* Information on the *tariqah* in late Ottoman Egypt is found in Tawfiq al-Tawil, *al-Tasawwuf fi Misr Iban al-ᶜAsr al-ᶜUthmani* (Sufism in Egypt During the Ottoman Era), (Cairo, 1950), I, 36-51; and F. de Jong, *Turuq and Turuq-Linked Institutions in Nineteenth Century Egypt,* (Leiden, 1978), henceforth *Turuq.*

7. *Rise of Colleges,* 10.

8. *Islamic Society,* I, pt. 2, 183.

9. *Rise of Colleges*, 291.

10. On *Shaikh al-Islam,* see J. H. Kramers, "Seyh Ul-Islam" in T. Yazici, S. Buluc, F. Isiltan, N. M. Cetin, A. Karahan, O. F. Koprulu, eds. *Islam Ansiklopedisi,* (Istanbul, 1970), 11, 485-489; and Norman Itzkowitz, "Men and Ideas in the Eighteenth Century Ottoman Empire" in Thomas Naff & Roger Owen, eds., *Studies in Eighteenth Century Islamic History,* (Carbondale & Edwardsville, 1977), 17. See also, Richard Repp, "The Altered Nature and Role of the Ulama" in *ibid,* 277-287.

11. J. R. Walsh, "Fatwa" in *EI2.*

12. *Islamic Society,* I, pt. 2, 99-100. On the distinct nature of the relationship between religious scholars and the Mamluks, see Afaf Lutfi el-Sayed [Marsot], "The Role of the Ulama in Egypt During the Early Nineteenth Century" in P. M. Holt, ed., *Political and Social Change in Modern Egypt,* (London, 1968), 265-266, henceforth, *Role of the Ulama;* and Afaf Lutfi al-Sayyid [now Marsot], "The Wealth of the Ulama in Late Eighteenth Century Cairo" in Thomas Naff & Roger Owen, eds., *Studies in Eighteenth Century Islamic History,* (Carbondale & Edwardsville, 1977), 206-207, henceforth, *Wealth of the Ulama.* See also Sherman A. Jackson, *In Defense of Two-Tired Orthodoxy,* (Doctorate Dissertation, University of Pennsylvania, 1991) for important insights on the status of religious scholars in Ayyubid-Mamluk Egypt.

13. On the guilds of merchants and artisans in late Ottoman Egypt, see Abd al-Rahman al-Rafici, *Tarikh al-Harakah al-Qawmiyyah wa-Tatawwur Nizam al-Hukm fi Misr,* (Cairo, 1981, [first published 1928]), I, 64-65, henceforth *Qawmiyyah;* and references throughout *Egyptian Guilds.*

14. *Islamic Society,* I, pt. 2, 77, 79, 183-184.

15. Abd al-Rahman al-Jabarti, *cAja'ib al-Athar fi al-Tarajim wa-al-Akhbar* (The Marvelous Events that Occurred in Biographies and Accounts), (Cairo, 1958), II, 166-167, henceforth *cAja'ib al-Athar.*

16. *Ibid,* 167.

17. (Approx.) 25,000 artisans + (approx.) 9000 merchants = 59.6% of (approx.) 57,000, the total adult male population, excluding slaves. The approximations appear in *Qawmiyyah,* 1,70. (Calculations are mine).

18. The accounts are found in *cAja'ib al-Athar,* II, 218-223; Niqula al-Turk, *Dhikr Tamaluk Jumhur al-Faransawiyyah bi-al-Aqtar al-Misriyyah wa-al-Bilad al-Shamiyyah* (The Account of the French Campaign on Egypt and Syria), (Beirut, 1990 [first published in 1839]), 58-61, henceforth *Dhikr Tamaluk;* and H. Charles Lavauzelle, ed., C. La Jonquiere, *L'Expedition francaise en Egypte* (1798-1801), I-V, (Paris, 1899-1907), III, 279, henceforth *L'Expedition francaise.*

19. *cAja'ib al-Athar,* II, 325-326, 327, respectively.

20. *Qawmiyyah,* II, 156-159.

21. On Muhammad Ali, see Afaf Lutfi al-Sayyid Marsot, *Egypt in the Reign of Muhammad Ali* (Cambridge, 1984), 24-35, henceforth *Reign of Muhammad Ali.* On his agreement with Cairo's religious scholars, see *cAja'ib al-Athar,* III, 62-63.

22. *Ibid,* III, 64-82.

23. The findings appear in *Role of the Ulama, Turuq, Egyptian Guilds*, and Gabriel Baer, *Studies in the Social History of Modern Egypt* (Chicago, 1969), 79, henceforth, *Social History of Modern Egypt*.

24. *Social History of Modern Egypt*, 79.

25. *Islamic Society,* I, pt. 2, 175.

26. *Role of the Ulama*, 270.

27. *Turuq*, 3.

28. *Ibid*, 22-23.

29. *Ibid*, 201-203, 204-205, 205-214, respectively.

30. *Role of the Ulama,* 278; and *Egyptian Guilds,* 149.

31. *Egyptian Guilds,* 78-79.

32. *Role of the Ulama,* 279.

33. A Muslim who abides by the authority of twelve consecutive descendants of the Prophet. The *shiᶜah* are found mostly in Iraq and Iran.

34. A Muslim who abides by the authority of one of four guilds/schools of law. Presently, the majority of Muslims are *Sunni*.

35. On al-Afghani's life and activities, see Muhammad al-Makhzumi, *Khatirat Jamal al-Din al-Afghani* (The Reflections of Jamal al-Din al-Afghani), (Beirut, 1931), 25-62, henceforth *Khatirat al-Afghani*; Muhammad Rashid Rida, *Tarikh al-Ustadh al-Imam Muhammad ᶜAbduh* (Biography of the Teacher, the Imam, Muhammad Abduh), (Cairo, 1931), I, 27-91, henceforth *Tarikh ᶜAbduh*; "al-Sayyid Jamal al-Din al-Husayni al-Afghani," in Jurji Zaydan, ed., *Majallat al-Hilal* (The Journal of The Crescent), (Cairo, 1892-[still published], V, 567; and N. R. Keddie, *Sayyid Jamal al-Din "al-Afghani": A Political Biography,* (Berkeley, 1972), henceforth *al-Afghani.*

36. On al-Afghani's views, see *Tarikh ᶜAbduh,* I, 33-34, 73-84; *Kharirat al-Afghani,* 72-79; and N. R. Keddie, *An Islamic Response to Imperialism,* (Berkeley, 1983), 36-97, henceforth *Islamic Response.*

37. On the evolution of the concept of civil society in the West, see J. Keane, "Despotism and Democracy" in J. Keane, ed., *Civil Society and the State–New European Perspectives* (London & New York: 1988), 39-50, henceforth *Despotism and Democracy*. For arguments in support of the use of the term 'civil society' to Muslim countries, see Rachid al-Ghannouchi, Tunisia: *The Islamic Movement and Civil Society* at http://www.ghannouchi.net. For arguments to the contrary, see E. Gellner, *Conditions of Liberty, Civil Society and its Rivals* (London, 1994), 43.

38. Muhammad Amarah, ed., *al-Aᶜmal al-Kamilah li-al-Imam Muhammad ᶜAbduh* (The Complete Works of Muhammad Abduh), (Beirut, 1972), I, 479-480, henceforth *Aᶜmal ᶜAbduh.*

39. Jurji Zaydan, *Tarikh al-Masuniyyah al-ᶜAmm,* (Cairo, 1889), 210-220, henceforth *Tarikh al-Masuniyyah*; and Jacob M. Landau, "Prolegomena to a study of Secret Societies in Modern Egypt," in *Middle Eastern Studies,* I, No. 2 (January, 1965), 141, henceforth *Secret Societies.*

40. A general treatment of Muhammad Ali's achievements and failures is found in *Egypt in the Reign of Muhammad Ali.*

41. On the Egyptian setting during the reign of Khedive Ismail, see Abd al-Rahman al-Rafi^{c}i, *^{c}Asr Ismail,* (Cairo, 1932), 1,72; *ibid*, II, 266, 302-320, 323-332, henceforth *^{c}Asr Isma^{c}il*; and David S. Landes, *Bankers and Pashas: International Finance and Economic Imperialism in Egypt,* (Cambridge, 1958), 128-146, henceforth *Bankers and Pashas.*

42. *Tarikh ^{c}Abduh,* I, 32-33,40; and Albert A. Kudsi-Zadeh, "Afghani and Freemasonry in Egypt" in *Journal of the American Oriental Society,* Vol. 92, No. 1, (January-March, 1972), 25, henceforth "al-Afghani and Freemasonry".

43. On the use of his home see *Tarikk ^{c}Abduh*, I, 32, 44. On the stone throwing incident, see "al-Afghani and Freemasonry," 25. On the subsequent utilization of coffee shops, see *Tarikh ^{c}Abduh,* I, 42, 44. On how coffee shops were perceived in late nineteenth century Cairo, see Muhammad Abduh's comment in *Tarikh ^{c}Abduh,* I, 35.

44. On al-Afghani's circles of knowledge, see *Tarikh ^{c}Abduh,* I, 25-26, 32, 44-45.

45. *Tarikh ^{c}Abduh,* I, 25-27.

46. *Tarikh ^{c}Abduh.* I, 44-46; *ibid*, I, 25-26; *ibid*, I, 26, 48-49; *A^{c}mal ^{c}Abduh,* 1, 482; and *al-Afghani,* 95, respectively.

47. A. D. al-Jumayi, *^{c}Abd Allah al-Nadim,* (Cairo, 1980) 43, henceforth *^{c}Abd Allah al-Nadim*; and *Tarikh ^{c}Abduh,* I, 25, 45, 46, 138, 46, 138, 595, 955, 132, 1043, 1052, 603, 46, respectively.

48. Jacob Landau, "Abu Naddara an Egyptian Jewish Nationalist" in *The Journal of Jewish Studies,* III, (1952), 30-44, henceforth *Abu Naddara.*

49. Awni Ishaq, ed., *al-Durar* (The Pearls), (Beirut, 1909) 5-15, henceforth *al-Durar*; and *Tarikh ^{c}Abduh,* I, 45, 31, respectively.

50. "Jaridah" in *Da'irat al-Ma^{c}arif al-Islamiyyah* (The Encyclopedia of Islam, Arabic Edition), (Cairo, n.d.), XI, 246, henceforth *Ma^{c}arif.*

51. *Ibid*, 246, 266.

52. *^{c}Asr Isma^{c}il,* II, 247-248; and Filib di Tarrazi, *Tarikh al-Sahafah al-^{c}Arabiyyah* (History of Arab Journalism), (Beirut, 1913), I, 69, henceforth *Tarikh al-Sahafah.*

53. *^{c}Asr Isma^{c}il*, 248; and *Tarikh al-Sahafah*, I, 277.

54. See, for example, *Tarikh ^{c}Abduh,* I, 32.

55. *Tarikh ^{c}Abduh,* I, 38.

56. *Abu Naddara,* 30-44. On the possible influence of the clandestine journals of European secret associations on *Abu Nazzarah Zarqa',* see *Secret Societies,* 141.

57. Sadir (Publishing House), ed., *Suhuf Abu Nazzarah, 1878-1900,* (The Journals of Abu Nazzarah, 1878-1900), (Beirut, n.d.), (Year 1878-1879), 30.

58. *Tarikh ^{c}Abduh,* I, 45.

59. Ali Shalash, ed., *Jamal al-Din al-Afghani: al-ᶜAmal al-Majhulah* (Jamal al-Din al-Afghani: The Unknown Works), (London, 1987), 76, henceforth *Aᶜmal al-Afghani al-Majhulah.*

60. *Al-Afghani,* 97-98.

61. *Tarikh ᶜAbduh*, I, 46-48.

62. Jacob M. Landau, *Parliaments and Parties in Egypt* (Tel Aviv, 1953), 101-103, henceforth *Parliaments.*

63. Albert Kudsi-Zadeh, "Political Journalism in Egypt" in *The Muslim World,* Vol. LXX, No. 1, (January, 1980), 53-54, henceforth *Political Journalism*; and *Parliaments,* 102-103.

64. *Al-Afghani*, 98.

65. *Aᶜmal al-Afghani al-Majhulah,* 76-82.

66. *Tarikh al-Masuniyyah,* 211. See also, Robert Freke Gould, *The History of Freemasonry,* (London, 1887), III, 340.

67. *Tarikh al-Masuniyyah*, 211.

68. *Secret Societies*, 139.

69. *Ibid.*

70. *Tarikh al-Masuniyyah*, 212-213.

71. *Ibid*, 218-219.

72. *Ibid*, 220.

73. "al-Afghani and Freemasonry", 28.

74. See the short, yet highly informative, "al-Jamᶜiyyat fi al-Islam" in *al-Hilal,* XXXVI, (April, 1, 1918), 605.

75. Iraj Afshar and Asghar Mahdavi, eds., *Majmuᶜyi Asnad va Madarik-i Jap Nishuda Darbara-yi Jamal al-Din Mashhur bi Afghani* (A Collection of Previously Unpublished Documents and Notes Concerning Jamal al-Din, better known as al-Afghani), (Tehran, 1963), Plate 16, photo: 40, henceforth *Documents.*

76. *Documents*, 15.

77. On *Ikhwan al-Safa'*, see *EI2.*

78. *al-Ismaᶜiliyyah* is a branch of *Shiᶜi* Islam characterized by its philosophical and esoteric tendencies.

79. *Documents,* 24, No. 60, containing an invitation from the Italian lodge *Luce d'Oriente* and Dated 1877.

80. As indicated by *Documents,* 24, No. 63, containing an invitation to the Italian *Mazzini* lodge and the Italian *Nilo* lodge and Dated 1878; and *ibid*, 25, No. 68, containing an invitation to attend the *Mazzini* lodge and dated February 5, 1879. Al-Afghani was deported in late August 1879.

81. *Documents,* 24, No 59.

82. *Ibid*, Plate 16, photo: 41.

83. *Ibid*, 24, No. 59, dated January, 24, 1878, containing an invitation to attend an extraordinary session to *Kawkab al-Sharq*; *ibid*, 24, No. 64, dated May, 15, 1878, containing an invitation to an extraordinary session to *Kawkab al-Sharq*; *ibid*, 25, No. 67, dated October, 17,1878, containing an invitation to a session in Alexandria to *Kawkab al-Sharq*; and *ibid*, 25, No. 70, containing a letter from *Kawkab al-Sharq*.

84. *Documents,* 24, No. 61, No. 65, 25, No. 66, No. 69, respectively. On *al-Nil* and *Grecia*, see "Afghani and Freemasonry", 27.

85. Mohammed Sabry, *La genese de l'esprit national egyptien (1863-82)* (The Genesis of the National Egyptian Spirit), (Paris, 1924), henceforth *La genese.*

86. *La genese,* 143; *Khatirat al-Afghani,* 44; and *Tarikh ᶜAbduh*, I, 41-42,46, respectively.

87. "Afghani and Freemasonry", 27.

88. *Ibid.*

89. *Ibid*, 30.

90. "Afghani and Freemasonry", 30, note: 55.

91. *Tarikh ᶜAbduh,* I, 40; and *Khatirat al-Afghani*, 44, respectively.

92. Rida bases his information on a discussion he had with Abduh, and, though he does not specify a date, he states that al-Afghani withdrew when the Prince of Wales visited Egypt; an event known to have taken place in 1876. See Rashid Rida, ed., *Majallat al-Manar* (The Journal of the Beacon), (1898-1935), VIII, 402-403, henceforth *Manar.*

93. A. H. Hourani, "Djamᶜiyyah" in *EI2*.

94. Monroe Berger, *Islam in Egypt Today: Social and Political Aspects of Popular Religion* (Cambridge, 1970), 5-6, henceforth *Islam in Egypt Today.*

95. Jurji Zaydan, *Tarikh Adab al-Lughah al-ᶜArabiyyah,* (History of Arabic Literature), (Cairo, 1957), IV, 77-80, henceforth *Tarikh Adab.*

96. Juan R. I. Cole, *Colonialism and Revolution in the Middle East* (Princeton, 1992), 153-154, henceforth *Colonialism and Revolution*; Alexander Scholch, *Egypt for the Egyptians: The Sociopolitical Crisis in Egypt, 1878-1882* (London, 1981), 112-114, henceforth *Egypt for the Egyptians*; and E. Kedourie, "Hizb" in *EI2.*

97. A. H. Hourani, "Djamᶜiyyah" in *EI2*; and *Parliaments*, 101-103.

98. *Colonialism and Revolution,* 157. A general treatment of benevolent associations in Egypt during this period is found in *Islam in Egypt Today,* 90-126.

99. *Tarikh ᶜAbduh*, I, 102-103.

100. *Parliaments*, 22-25.

101. Irene L. Gendzier, *The Practical Visions of Yaqub Sannu* (Cambridge, 1966), 31, henceforth *Practical Visions.*

102. *Abu Naddara*, 32-33.

103. *Kharirat al-Afghani*, 44-45.

104. *Tarikh ᶜAbduh*, I, 40

105. On the organized activity of the military branch of this movement, headed by Ahmad Urabi, see *Secret Societies,* 143-147.

106. *Ibid*, 77.

107. *Ibid*, 74-75. See also, *Documents,* Plate 13, photos: 34-35.

108. *Al-Afghani*, 114; and Elie Kedourie, *Afghani and Abduh: An Essay on Religious Unbelief and Political Activism in Modern Islam* (New York, 1966), 25, henceforth *Afghani and Abduh.*

109. See Wilfred S. Blunt, *Secret History of the English Occupation of Egypt,* (New York, 1922), 369, henceforth *Secret History.* Though it is N. Keddie who points out that Blunt's statement in regard to al-Afghani's visit to America has no historical basis (see *al-Afghani,* 183), thereby casting doubt on his credibility, she does not, however, question the accuracy of his report on the assassination plot (see *al-Afghani,* 114).

110. *Al-Afghani*, 404-421.

111. *Documents,* Plate 13, photo: 35-36.

112. *Tarikh ᶜAbduh*, I, 33, 76. Note: no explicit evidence has as yet been unearthed explicitly documenting the role of the British and/or French consul in al-Afghani's ouster from Egypt.

113. *Tarikh ᶜAbduh*, I, 33, 76; and *Khatirat al-Afghani, 50.*

114. Naji Allush, ed., *Adib Ishaq, al-Kitabat al-Siyasiyyah wa-al-Ijtimaᶜiyyah* (Adib Ishaq, The Political and Social Works), (Beirut, 1978), 12, henceforth *Adib.*

115. *Al-Afghani,* 118-119; and "al-Afghani and Freemasonry", 33.

116. *Al-Afghani,* 113.

117. *Ibid*, 121-122.

118. A. M. Broadly, *How We Defended Arabi and His Friends: A Story of Egypt and the Egyptians* (London, 1884), 262, henceforth *Arabi and His Friends.* Note, this work is regarded as credible and has been used by important studies on al-Afghani. See, for example, *Secret Societies,* 176; and *Afghani and Abduh,* 12.

119. On al-Afghani's turn towards strong public speeches shortly prior to his deportation, see *al-Afghani,* 118. Excerpts of al-Afghani's speeches are found in *TarikhᶜAbduh,* I, 46-47.

120. Arthur Goldschmidt, Jr., *Modern Egypt,* (Colorado, 1988), 46.

121. Yunan Labib Rizq, *al-Hayat al-Hizbiyyah fi Misr fi ᶜAhd al-Ihtilal al-Britani,* 1882-1914 (Political Life in Egypt During the British Occupation: 1882-1914), (Cairo, 1970), 14, henceforth, *Hizbiyyah.*

122. To be henceforth referred to as *Waqa'iᶜ.*

123. Biographical information on Muhammad Abduh is found in *Tarikh ᶜAbduh,* I-III. Other sources include, Adams, *Islam and Modernism*; Malcolm H. Kerr, *Islamic*

Reform: The Political and Legal Theories of Muhammad Abduh and Rashid Rida, (Berkeley and Los Angeles, 1966), henceforth *Theories of Abduh and Rida*; Osman Amin, *Muhammad Abduh,* Charles Wendell, trans., (Washington, D.C., 1953), henceforth *Muhammad Abduh;* Muhammad Amarah, *al-Imam Muhammad ᶜAbduh Mujadid al-Dunyah bi-Tajdid al-Din* (Muhammad Abduh: The Reformer of the Affairs of the World through Reforming Religion), (Beirut, 1985), henceforth *Mujadid al-Dunyah*; Abd al-Halim al-Jundi, *al-Imam Muhammad ᶜAbduh,* (Cairo, n.d.), henceforth *al-Imam Muhammad ᶜAbduh*; and J. Schacht, "Muhammad Abduh" in *EI2*. See also Suhail Ibn Salim Hanna's article "Scholarship and Muhammad Abduh" in which problems associated with biographical works on Abduh are addressed: *The Muslim World,* LIX, Nos. 3-4, (July-October, 1969), 300-307.

124. *Aᶜmal Abduh,* I, 36.

125. *Tarikh ᶜAbduh*, I, 175.

126. *Ibid*, I, 137, 175.

127. The report is reproduced in *ibid*, I, 176-177.

128. *Ibid*, I, 138.

129. *Tarikh ᶜAbduh*, I, 148.

130. On Abduh's harassment by Egyptian officers, see *ibid*, I, 146. Note: Abduh's role in the Urabi Revolt is addressed below.

131. *Ibid*, II, 56.

132. An interesting debate on when this antithesis between 'authentic' and 'historical' Islam was first arrived at by al-Afghani and Abduh appeared in *The Muslim World*. While M. Milson argued that it was already conceptualized at the time al-Afghani responded to Renan (March, 1883), E. Kedourie argued that it was much later. See Menahem Milson, "The Elusive Jamal al-Din al-Afghani" in *The Muslim World,* (October, 1968), No. 4, 295-307; E Kedourie, "The Elusive Jamal al-Din al-Afghani: A Comment" & Menaham Milson "The Elusive Jamal al-Din al-Afghani: A Rejoinder" in *The Muslim World,* (July-October, 1969), Nos. 3-4, 308-314 & 315-316, respectively. Neither seems to be aware of a number of articles that were published in *Waaʾiᶜ* in which Abduh made the distinction between a 'historical and authentic' Islam. See, for example, "Hukm al-Shariᶜah fi Taᶜdud al-Zawjat" (The Position of Islamic Religious Law on Polygamy), (March 8,1881), reprinted in *Aᶜmal ᶜAbduh*, II, 78-83; and "ᶜAdat al-Ma'atim" (Common Practices Associated With Funerals), (June 8,1881), reprinted in *ibid*, 143-147.

133. A. Merad "Islah" in *EI2*.

134. *Aᶜmal ᶜAbduh,* I, 727.

135. "Ibtal al-Bidaᶜ Min Nazarat al-Awqaf al-ᶜUmumiyyah" (The Abrogation of Innovations By the Ministry of Public Charitable Trusts) in *Waqa'iᶜ,* No. 958, (November, 1880), reprinted in *Aᶜmal ᶜAbduh*, II, 23-26.

136. "Tanbih Rasmi: Butlan al-Dawsah" (An Official Proclamation: The Abrogation of al-Dawsah) in *Waqa'iᶜ,* No. 1038 (February, 1881), reprinted in *ibid*, II, 53-55; and "al-Dawsah" in *Waqa'iᶜ,* No. 1078 (April, 1881), reprinted in *ibid*, II, 56-59.

137. *Ibid*, II, 54.

138. *Ibid.*

139. *Ibid*, II, 55.

140. "Hajat al-Insan ila al-Zawaj" (The Human Need for Marriage) in *Waqa'i*, No. 1055, (March, 1881), reprinted in *ibid*, II, 68-71; "Hukm al-Shari^cah fi Ta^cdud al-Zawjat" (The Position of Islamic Religious Law on Polygamy), in *Waqa'i*, No. 1056, (March,1881), reprinted in *A^cmal ^cAbduh*, II, 78-83; "Fawa'id al-Musaharah" (The Benefits of Marrying into Another Family) in *Waqa'i*, No. 1059, (March, 1881), reprinted in *ibid*, II, 96-99.

141. *Ibid*, II, 80.

142. "^cAwa'id al-Afrah" (Common Practices Associated With Weddings) in *Waqa'i*, No. 1116, (May, 1881), reprinted in *ibid*, II, 102-103.

143. "Fi al-Shura wa al-Istibdad" (On Constitutionalism and Authoritarianism) in *Waqa'i*, No 1279 (December, 1881), reprinted in *ibid*, I, 353.

144. *Ibid*, I, 352.

145. *Ibid*, I, 353.

146. *Ibid.*

147. See Ali Abd al-Qadir, "al-Qada' wa-al-Hisbah" in *Mausu^cat al-Hadarah al-Islamiyyah* (The Encyclopedia of Islamic Civilization), (Beirut, 1986), 271-287.

148. *A^cmal ^cAbduh*, I, 356.

149. See, J. R. Walsh, "Fatwa" in *EI2*.

150. On Abbasi al-Mahdi, see Said Ismail Ali, *Al-Azhar ^cAla Masrah al-Siyasah al-Misriyyah* (Al-Azhar On the Stage of Egyptian Politics), (Cairo, 1974), 182-183; henceforth *al-Azhar ^cAla Masrah al-Siyasah.*

151. *A^cmal ^cAbduh*, I, 506-512.

152. Roger Allen, *A Period of Time*, (Reading, 1992), 137, henceforth *A Period of Time*. On Muhammad al-Muwaylihi's relationship with Abduh, see *ibid*, 2-3, 101.

153. Abd al-Rahman al-Rafi^ci, *al-Thawrah al-^cUrabiyyah wa-al-Ihtilalal-Injilizi* (The Urabi Revolution and the British Occupation), (Cairo, 1966), 104-105, henceforth *al-Thawrah al-^cUrabiyyah.*

154. *Ibid*, 136-145.

155. "al-Quwah wa-al-Qanun" (Power and the Law) in *Waqa'i*, No 1031, (February, 1881), reprinted in *A^cmal ^cAbduh*, I, 285.

156. *Al-Thawrah al-^cUrabiyyah*, 133-145.

157. *Ibid*, 145.

158. On the 'Dual Proclamation', see *al-Thawrah al-^cUrabiyyah*, 214-215.

159. *Tarikh ^cAbduh*, I, 265.

160. On Abduh and nationalist conferences, see Alexander Scholch, *Egypt for the Egyptians: The Sociopolitical Crisis in Egypt, 1878-1882,* (London, 1981), 202, 205, 223, 263, 265, 270-271, henceforth *Egypt for the Egyptians*. On Abduh and the Program of the Nationalist Party, see *Secret History,* 132-133.

161. "Mahdar al-Istijwab" (The Investigation Report), reprinted in *A^cmal ^cAbduh,* I, 463-465.

162. *Ibid,* I, 465.

163. *Ibid.*

164. *Egypt for the Egyptians,* 189.

165. *Ibid,* 90, 350.

166. *Ibid,* 272-283, 288, 294.

167. In addition to "Mahdar al-Istijwab", see *Afghani and Abduh,* 35.

168. To be henceforth referred to as *^cUrwah.*

169. On al-Afghani's stay in India, see *al-Afghani,* 143-181.

170. In addition to utilizing the French against the British, al-Afghani tried to use the Russians against the British (*al-Afghani,* 305), and the British against the Russians (*al-Afghani,* 250-251).

171. *Documents,* photos: 42-43.

172. On *al-Nahlah,* see *Tarikh al-Sahafah,* II, 253. On *al-Basir,* see *ibid,* II, 259-260. On *Abu Nazzarah,* see *ibid,* II, 254-256.

173. *Al-Basir* (No. 3, Year V, 1882), reprinted in *A^cmal al-Afghani al-Majhulah,* 84-84, 85-87, respectively; *al-Nahlah,* (February 8,1883), (April 5, 1883), (April 26, 1883), and (May 3,1883), reprinted in Shalash, *A^cmal al-Afghani al-Majhulah,* 89-90, 100-106, 107-110, 111-114, respectively; and *Abu Nazzarah* (January, 1883) and (February, 1883), reprinted in *A^cmal al-Afghani al-Majhulah,* 88, 91-100, respectively.

174. The article was published in *L'Intransigeant* on April 24, 1883 as "Lettre sur l'Hindoustan" (A Letter on India) and is reprinted in *Afghani and Abduh,* 70-74. According to *al-Basir* (*A^cmal al-Afghani al-Majhula,* 100) extracts of this article were also published in the *Standard, Daily Telegraph, Globe,* and *Daily News,* and the Austrian *Neue Freie Presse.*

175. "Réponse à Renan" appeared in *Journal des Debats* on May 18,1883. See *al-Afghani,* 189. The articles in *L'Intransigeant* date December 8,1883, December 11, 1883, and December 17,1883, respectively; and are reprinted by *Afghani and Abduh,* 74-79,79-83, and 83-86, respectively.

176. Abduh wrote two letters to al-Afghani from Beirut (March 14, and June 14, 1883). Both are found in *Documents,* 63-64, photos 134-137, and 64-65, photos: 138-140, respectively.

177. *^cUrwah*'s articles are reprinted in Muhammad Amarah, ed., *Jamal al-Din al-Afghani: al-A^cmal al-Siyasiyyah* (Jamal al-Din al-Afghani: The Political Works), (Beirut, 1979), henceforth *A^cmal al-Afghani.* On references to *Republique Francaise,*

see *A^cmal al-Afghani,* 116, 207, 226, 228; to *Matin,* 90, 114, 175, 181, 195, 217, 219, 233, 243, 256, 259-260; to *Debat,* 207; to *Daily News,* 43, 154, 176, 212, 222, 245, 247, 254, 258, 260; to *Daily Telegraph,* 114, 209, 233, 251, 258; to *Morning Post,* 210; to *Pall Mall Gazette,* 116, 154, 196, 219; to *Post,* 107; to *Standard,* 88, 90, 137, 176, 247, 250; and to *Times,* 103-104, 108-109, 149, 175, 195, 206, 209-210, 213, 216, 224, 229, 242-243, 254, 256, 257, 260.

178. In an article to *Paris* (December 5,1884), al-Afghani acknowledged that he had hired a number of interpreters. The article is reprinted in Homa Pakdman, *Djamal ed-Din Asad Abadi dit Afghani,* (Paris, 1969), 360-361, henceforth *Abadi.*

179. On Bavanati's cooperation in producing *^cUrwah,* see *Tarikh ^cAbduh,* I, 817-819. On the cooperation of Sannu, see *Abu Naddara,* 39-40.

180. *Documents,* pl. 46, photo: 100; and *A Period of Time,* 5.

181. The table is based on a summary of the notebook made by Pakdman in *Abadi,* 100-101, and other relevant material, photographed and/or described in *Documents.*

182. Though the notebook summarized by *Abadi* does not contain information on *^cUrwah*'s circulation in Iran, a number of documents attest to its arrival in Iranian cities. See *Documents,* 28, doc. nos. 84, 91; 30, doc. no. 106; 32, doc. no. 32; and 33, doc. no. 113.

183. A number of documents also attest to the arrival of *^cUrwah* in Indian cities. See *ibid,* 30, doc. no. 136: 34, docs. no. 140-142.

184. A number of documents confirm the arrival of *^cUrwah* in Indonesian cities. See *ibid,* 63, doc. nos. 212, 214.

185. Issues were sent to the exiled Egyptian officers. See *ibid,* 55, doc. no. 173.

186. On *Itla^c, Farhang, Akhbar-e ^cAm,* see *^cUrwah* in *A^cmal al-Afghani,* 265, 269, 305, 307, respectively. On *Udah Akhbar* and *Bazar Partarka,* see *ibid,* 306.

187. On attempts to acquire funds from Prince Abd al-Halim, see the record of a letter dated January 18, 1884 from Abduh and one Muhammad Afandi al-Shubashi in Paris to Prince Abd al-Halim in Istanbul (*Documents,* 77). Abduh's letter on July 22, 1884 to an unidentified Muslim prince (*Tarikh ^cAbduh,* II, 581) seems to be also directed to Prince Abd al-Halim. On attempts to acquire funds from the ex. Khedive Ismail, General Husain, and Blunt, see articles in *Paris* (December 3, and 12, 1884) by an anonymous correspondent, reprinted in *Abadi,* 357-361. *Tarikh al-Sahafah,* II, 261 contains the only reference to Ahmad al-Minshawi's financial contributions to *^cUrwah* that I have been able to identify. I was, however, able to trace a reference in *Tarikh ^cAbduh* to Minshawi. Significantly, he is described by Rida as a figure who made significant contributions to various benevolent projects, including some sponsored by al-jam^ciyyah al-khayriyyah al-Islamiyyah (not to be confused with the one inspired by al-Afghani) in which Abduh was heavily involved. See *Tarikh ^cAbduh,* I, 946-947.

188. Ismail's refusal to continue funding *^cUrwah* is found in *Paris* (December 3), reprinted in *Abadi,* 360; General Husain's refusal is cataloged in *Documents,* pl. 62, doc. 205, preserved in the *Library of Parliament at Tehran,* and summarized in *al-Afghani,* 217; Blunt's is found in *Paris* (December 12), reprinted in *Abadi,* 364. There is no explicit documentation of either Abd al-Halim's or al-Minshawi's refusal to continue their support.

189. *Abadi,* 360, 364, respectively.

190. *Aᶜmal al-Afghani,* II, 8.

191. *Ibid,* II, 8.

192. A Persian translation of Abduh's letter is found in *Documents,* 63-64. The Arabic original is in the *Library of Parliament in Tehran.*

193. Also contained in *Tarikh ᶜAbduh,* I, 287-288.

194. *Tarikh ᶜAbduh,* I, 285-287. [Italics added]

195. After Abduh died, his older brother, Hamudah Abduh, gave Rida Abduh's personal papers. See, *Tarikh ᶜAbduh,* I, 2.

196. *Ibid,* I, 48.

197. *Aᶜmal al-Afghani,* 31.

198. 'Al-Mahdi' is the title by which the leader of the Sudanese resistance against the British in the late nineteenth century was known.

199. "Al-Mas'alah al-Misriyyah Dawliyyah" (The Egyptian Question is an International Question) in *ᶜUrwah,* (May, 22, 1884), reprinted in *Tarikh ᶜAbduh,* I, 347.

200. *Ibid.*

201. Hasan M. Jawharah and Umar al-Disuqi, eds., Abd al-Rahman al-Jabarti, *Mazhar al-Taqdis bi-Dhihab Dawlat al-Firansis* (The Reveleation of Glory Through the Termination of the French Occupation), (Cairo, 1969), 54, henceforth *Mazhar,* 54.

202. Al-Moncef al-Chenoufi, "*Masadir ᶜan Rihlatay al-Ustadh al-Imam al-Shaikh Muhammad ᶜAbduh ila Tunis*" (Sources on the Teacher, the Imam, the Shaykh Muhammad Abduh's Two Trips to Tunis) in *Hawliyat al-Jamiᶜah al-Tunisiyyah,* No. 3, (1966), henceforth *Masadir,* 85-89.

203. The last document attesting to the branch's existence is a letter from Abduh to al-Shadhili Ibn Farhat on November 30,1885. See (letter no. 12) in *Tarikh ᶜAbduh,* II, 562; and *Masadir,* 90.

204. *Tarikh ᶜAbduh,* I, 84.

205. *Ibid,* I, 379-382.

206. Ali Shalash, *Muhammad ᶜAbduh: al-Aᶜmal al-Majhulah* (Muhammad Abduh: The Unknown Works), (London, 1987), 22, henceforth *Aᶜmal ᶜAbduh al-Majhulah.*

207. *Ibid,* 33.

208. *Ibid,* 32-33.

209. Muhammad Rashid Rida, *al-Manar wa-al-Azhar* (Al-Manar and al-Azhar), (Cairo, 1935), 9-11, henceforth *al-Manar wa-al-Azhar.*

210. *Ibid,* 't'.

211. *Tarikh ᶜAbduh,* I, 500-504, 569-575.

212. *Ibid,* I, 516-517.

213. *Ibid*, I, 1018.

214. Biographical information on Rashid Rida is found in two primary sources: *Tarikh ᶜAbduh,* I; and *al-Manar wa-al-Azhar.* Important secondary sources include, *Islam and Modernism*; Muhammad Ahmad Darniqah, *al-Sayyid Muhammad Rashid Rida: Islahatuhu al-Itimaᶜiyyah wa-al-Diniyyah* (al-Sayyid Rashid Rida: His Social and Religious Reforms), (Tripoli, 1986), henceforth *al-Sayyid Rashid Rida1*; Husain al-Dannawi, *al-Sayyid Rashid Rida: Fikrahu, Nidalahu al-Siyasi* (al-Sayyid Rashid Rida: His Thought and Political Struggle), (Tripoli, 1983), henceforth *al-Sayyid Rashid Rida2;* Ahmad al-Sharabasi, *Rashid Rida Sahib al-Manar: ᶜAsruhu wa-Hayatuhu wa-Masadir Thaqqfatuhu,* (Rashid Rida, the Founder of al-Manar: His Age, His Life and the Sources of His Education), (Cairo, 1970), henceforth *Sahib al-Manar*; and *Theories of Abduh and Rida.*

215. *Tarikh ᶜAbduh,* I, 1002-1003.

216. *Ibid*, I, 1002.

217. *Ibid*, I, 766.

218. *Ibid*, I, 766-767.

219. *Ibid*, I, 1003-1004.

220. *Ibid*, I, 1003.

221. *Ibid*, I, 1007-1011.

222. *Manar,* I, 5.

223. *Ibid.*

224. *Ibid*, 3.

225. *Ibid.*

226. *Ibid.*

227. *Ibid*, I, 580, 1005-1006.

228. *Tarikh ᶜAbduh,* I, 1006.

229. *Ibid*, I, 1008.

230. Filib di Tarrazi in his authoritative *Tarikh al-Sahafah* ranks it fourth after *al-Muqtataf, al-Hilal,* and *al-Mashriq,* (IV, 174-175, note: 1).

231. *Manar,* I, 4.

232. Chronologically listed are the national origins of letters that were mailed to *Manar* requesting a religious legal verdict. Note: current national designations are used for the cities from which *Manar* received its letters.

233. Salah al-Din al-Munajjid & Yusuf Q. Khuri, eds. *Fatawa al-Imam Muhammad Rashid Rida* (The Religious Legal Verdicts of Muhammad Rashid Rida), (Beirut, 1970), I, 75; 1, 67; I, 34; I, 81; I, 55; I, 48; I, 294; I, 145; I, 136; I, 109; I, 373; II, 464; II, 186; I, 91; II, 580; II, 713; III, 1909; II, 709; II, 785; III, 855; III, 890; III, 1121; III, 1122; IV, 1205; III, 1152; IV, 1290; IV, 1525; V, 631; V, 2064; V, 2147; V, 2147; VI, 2302; VI, 2410; VI, 2449, respectively, henceforth *Fatawa Rida.*

234. *Tarikh ᶜAbduh,* I, 1003.

235. Muhammad Rashid Rida, *Tafsir al-Manar* (The Qur'anic Exegeses of Manar), (Cairo, 1954 [4th edition]), I, 12, henceforth *Tafsir al-Manar.*

236. *Ibid.*

237. *Ibid,* I, 14.

238. Muhammad Salih al-Marakishi, *Tafkir Muhammad Rashid Rida min khilal majallat al-Manar, 1898-1935* (The Thought of Muhammad Rashid Rida, As Derived From the Journal of al-Manar, 1898-1935), (Tunis, 1985), 39, (note: 37), henceforth *Tafkir Rida.*

239. *Ibid.*

240. *Ibid,* 68.

241. A detailed discussion of this principle is found in *Islam and Modernism,* 127-132.

242. *Tafsir al-Manar,* I, 250.

243. See Hasan Hanafi, "al-ᶜAql wa-al-naql" in *Mausuᶜat al-Hadarah al-Islamiyyah* (The Encyclopedia of Islamic Civilization), (Beirut, 1986), I, 101-127.

244. *Tarikh ᶜAbduh,* I, 602.

245. See, for example, *Manar,* II, 577-582, 593-598, 609-612, 625-628, 648-651, 663-666; and III, 32-34, 221-225, 256-260.

246. *Tafkir Rida,* 229, note: 53.

247. *Ibid,* 235, note: 81.

248. *Fatawa Rida,* I, 79, 84, 127, 133, 223, respectively.

249. *Al-Manar wa al-Azhar,* 'h'-'k'.

250. *Ibid,* 9-16.

251. *Ibid,* 201-204.

252. *Tarikh ᶜAbduh,* I,

253. *Al-Manar wa-al-Azhar,* 12.

254. *Ibid.*

255. *Ibid,* 12-13, 15.

256. *Ibid,* 256-257.

257. *Ibid.*

258. *Ibid,* 286-296.

259. Note: *al-Ikhwan al-Muslimun* will be henceforth referred to as *Ikhwan.*

260. See *Islam in Egypt Today,* 90-126.

261. See 'Chapter 2'.

262. "*Hukumatuna wa-al-Jamᶜiyyat al-Khayriyyah*" (Our Government and Benevolent Associations) in *Waqa'iᶜ,* No. 942, (October, 1880), reprinted in *Aᶜmal ᶜAbduh,* II, 7-9.

263. *Tarikh Adab,* IV, 72; Linda S. Schilcher, *The Islamic Maqased of Beirut,* (American University of Beirut, 1969, Unpublished M. A. Thesis); and A. H. Hourani, "Djamnyyah" in *EI2.*

264. The accounts are written by eyewitnesses of Abduh's career in Beirut and are included by Rida in *Tarikh ʿAbduh,* I, 393-412.

265. On Arslan's relationship with Abduh, see Shakib Arslan, *al-Amir Shakib Arslan, Sirah Dhatiyyah* (Prince Shakib Arslan: A Personal Memoir), (Beirut, 1969), 29-32, henceforth *Shakib Arslan.*

266. *Tarikh ʿAbduh,* I, 726-752.

267. On the association's various successful projects, see *al-Imam Muhammad ʿAbduh,* 58-75.

268. See 'Chapter 3'.

269. On Shubli Numani, see Mehr Afroz Murad, *Intellectual Modernism of Shubli Numani, An Exposition of His Religious and Political Ideas,* (Lahore, 1976). On *Nadwat al-ʿUlama,* see *Manar,* IV, 279-280; and Muhammad Salih al-Marakishi, "Ta'thir Rashid Rida Fi Baʿd al-Bildan al-Islamiyyah, Maghriban wa Sharqan" (The Impact of The Thought of Rashid Rida on Some Muslim Countries in the West and East), in *Hawliyyat al-Jamiʿah al-Tunisiyyah,* (1985), No. 24, 93-95, henceforth *Ta'thir Rida.*

270. On *al-Jamʿiyyah al-Khalduniyyah,* see *Manar,* I, 817-822; and II, 318-320; Muhammad al-Fadil Ibn Ashur, *al-Harakah al-Adabiyyah wa-al-Fikriyyah Fi Tunis* (The Literary and Intellectual Movement in Tunis), (Tunis, 1972), 172-177, henceforth *al-Harakah al-Adabiyyah; Masadir,* 90-92; and Arnold H. Green, *The Tunisian Ulama, 1873-1915: Social Structure and Response to Ideological Currents,* (Leiden, 1978), 167-168,177, 184, henceforth *Tunisian Ulama.*

271. *Manar,* X, 342-343.

272. On Rida and *Shams al-Islam,* see *Manar,* II, 430-431, 438, 589-592, 703-704, 720, 765-766; and III, 89, 93, 120, 190.

273. *Ibid,* XVIII, 313-314.

274. *Tarikh Adab,* IV, 76, 72.

275. Yusuf Ibish, ed., *Rihlat al-Imam Muhammad Rashid Rida* (The Trips of al-Imam Muhammad Rashid Rida), (Beirut, 1971), 27, henceforth *Rihlat al-Imam.*

276. *Ibid,* 29.

277. *Manar,* XVII, 7-8.

278. *Rihlat al-Imam,* 45.

279. *Ibid,* 50.

280. On Rida's relationship with Tunisian religious scholars, see al-Moncef al-Chenoufi, "ʿAla'iq Rashid Rida Sahib Majallat al-Manar Maʿa al-Tunisiyyin, 1898-1935" (The Relationship between Rashid Rida, Founder of the Journal of al-Manar, and the Tunisians, 1898-1935) in *Hawliyyat al-Jamiʿah al-Tunisiyyah,* No. 4 (1967),

121-151, henceforth "Sahib Majallat al-Manar Ma{c}a al-Tunisiyyin". On Rida's visit to India, see *Rihlat al-Imam,* 77-86.

281. *A{c}mal {c}Abduh,* I, 707.

282. On how Abduh's conceptual approach to Islamic reform differed from that of al-Afghani, see for example, Rida, *Tarikh {c}Abduh,* I, 974-978.

283. *Ibid,* I, 974.

284. *Manar,* XI, 838.

285. *Manar,* I, 3.

286. See, for example, *Manar,* I, 250-252, 441-446, 808.

287. *Tarikh {c}Abduh,* I, 90. On Abu al-Huda's al-Sayyadi's relationship with Sultan Abd al-Hamid's, see B. Abu Maneh, "Sultan Abdulhamid II and Shaikh Abulhuda al-Sayyadi" in *Middle Eastern Studies* (May, 1979), XV, No. 2, 131-153.

288. *Tarikh {c}Abduh,* I, 1015.

289. *Manar,* XII, 12-13.

290. *Ibid,* XII, 13.

291. *Ibid.*

292. *Ibid,* XII, 13-14. In actuality, the C.U.P. allowed non-Muslims to join. Rida's perception of the C.U.P. appears to be based on the fact that non of its major leaders were Christians or Jews. See Bernard Lewis, *The Emergence of Modern Turkey* (Oxford, 1968), 211, note: 4.

293. *Manar,* XXVI, 293. See also, *ibid,* 291-292.

294. *Rihlat al-Imam,* 71.

295. See Muhammad Izzat Darwazah in *Nash'at al-Harakah al-{c}Arabiyyah al-Hadithah* (The Rise of the Modern Arab Movement), (Beirut, 1971), 295-398, henceforth *Nash'at.*

296. *See Manar,* XVI, 226-231; XVII, 234-239; and XXVI, 294-295.

297. *Ibid,* XVI, 294.

298. *Ibid,* XVI, 295.

299. *Ibid.*

300. *Ibid.*

301. George Antonius, *The Arab Awakening,* (Philadelphia, 1939), 109, note: 2, henceforth *Awakening.*

302. *Nash'at,* 360.

303. Amin Said, *Asrar al-Thawrah al-{c}Arabiyyah al-Kubra* (Secrets of the Great Arab Revolt), (Cairo, n.d.), 38, henceforth *Asrar.*

304. Amin Said, *al-Thawrah al-{c}Arabiyyah al-Kubra* (Cairo, n.d.), henceforth *Thawrah.*

305. *Nash'at,* 507.

306. *Manar,* XXVIII, 4-5, 470.

307. *Thawrah,* I, 49.

308. *Thawrah,* I, 50. Note: both ᶜAsir and Najd are currently located in Saudi Arabia.

309. *Thawrah,* I, 50. Note: Hijaz is currently located in Saudi Arabia.

310. On Rida's trip to India, see *Rihlat al-Imam,* 77-91.

311. *Ibid,* 87, 89, respectively.

312. On Rida's trip to Hijaz, see *ibid,* 92-210. On the pamphlet distribution incident, see Eliezer Tauber, "Rashid Rida As Pan-Arabist Before World War I" in *The Muslim World,* LXXIX. No. 2 (April, 1989), 109, (note: 18), henceforth *Pan-Arabist.*

313. Ali Sultan, *Tarikh Suriyyah,* 1908-1918 (The History of Syria, 1908-1918), (Damascus, 1987), 47, henceforth *Tarikh Suriyyah.*

314. *Ibid,* 47.

315. *Rihlat al-Imam,* 213.

316. *Ibid,* 311-384. Although Martin Kramer's, *Islam Assembled,* (New York, 1986), does not address this conference, it nevertheless contains important information and insights on the phenomenon of conferences organized by Muslim reformers.

317. *Rihlat al-Imam,* 356.

318. *Asrar,* 37-38.

319. Muhammad al-Misri, ed., Muhammad Kurd Ali, *al-Muᶜasirun* (Damascus, 1980), 336.

320. *Manar,* XXVIII, 788.

321. On *Jamᶜiyyat al-Shubban al-Muslimin,* see *Manar,* XXVIII, 788-792; and XXXI, 205-218; Hasan al-Banna, *Mudhakkarat al-Daᶜwah wa-al-Daᶜiyah* (Memoirs of the Message and of the Messenger), (Cairo, 1978), 58, 74, henceforth *Mudhakkarat;* Muhammad Muti al-Hafiz & Nizar Abazah, *Tarikh ᶜUlama' Dimashq fi al-Qarn al-Rabiᶜ ᶜAshar al-Hijri* (History of Damascene Religious Scholars in the Fourteenth Islamic Century [1882-1980]), (Damascus, 1986), II, 858-859, henceforth, *Tarikh ᶜUlama' Dimashq;* "Ta'thir Rida", 87; G. Kampffmayer, "Egypt and Western Asia" in H.A.R. Gibb, ed., *Whither Islam?,* (London, 1932), 101-170, henceforth "Egypt and Western Asia"; and James Heyworth-Dunne, *Religious and Political Trends in Modern Egypt,* (Washington, 1950), 11-14, henceforth *Religious and Political Trends.* Note: Kampffmayer's essay is based on his visit to the headquarters of *al-Shubban al-Muslimun* in Cairo and his interviewing of some of its primary figures.

322. *Manar,* XXVIII, 788.

323. On Abd al-Hamid Saᶜd, see, "Ta'thir Rida", 87. On Muhibb al-Din al-Khatib, see *Tarikh ᶜUlama Dimashq,* II, 847-862.

324. "Egypt and Central Asia", 105-106.

325. *Manar,* XXVIII, 789.

326. On *al-Nashrah,* see "Egypt and Central Asia", 114-119.

327. The articles of *Jam^ciyyat al-Shubban al-Muslimin*'s constitution are found in *Manar,* XXVIII, 788-792.

328. "Egypt and Central Asia", 121.

329. *Manar,* XXXI, 205.

330. "Egypt and Central Asia", 121-122.

331. On Rida's relationship with Syrian religious scholars, see *Rihlat al-Imam,* 9-53, 253-310; and *Islamic Reform,* 38, 56, 59-62. On *Jam^ciyyat al-Ulama',* see *Tarikh ^cUlama' Dimashq,* II, 660-666; Johannes Reissner, *Ideologie und Politik der Muslimbruder Syriens,* (Freiburg, 1980), 92-93, henceforth *Muslimbruder*; and Philip S. Khoury, *Syria and the French Mandate, The Politics of Arab Nationalism, 1920-1945,* (Princeton, 1987), 576, 608, henceforth *Syria and the French.*

332. *Tarikh ^cUlama' Dimashq,* II, 664.

333. On Rida's relationship with Algerian religious scholars, see "Ta'thir Rida", 74-78. On Ibn Badis, see Ammar al-Talibi, *Ibn Badis, Hayatuhu wa-Atharuhu* (Ibn Badis, His Life and Works), I-IV, (Algiers, 1968). On *Jam^ciyyat al-^cUlama' al-Muslimin,* see Ahmad al-Khatib, *Jam^ciyyat al-^cUlama' al-Muslimin al-Jaza'iriyin wa-Atharuha al-Islahi fi al-Jaza'ir* (The Association of Muslim Algerian Scholars and Its Reformist Impact on Algeria), (Algiers, 1985). On the Tunisian *al-Shubban al-Muslimun ,* see "Ta'thir Rida", 71. Note: although, the Tunisian *Shubban al-Muslimun* was inspired by its Egyptian model, they do not appear to have been linked administratively.

334. "Ta'thir Rida", 70-74, 76-78, respectively.

335. See Ali Ahmad, "Djam^ciyyah" in *EI2,* 437.

336. *Manar,* I, 664; and XXVIII, 788, respectively.

337. On the social standing of *Jam^ciyyat al-Shubban al-Muslimin*'s members, see *Islam in Egypt Today,* 126.

338. *Mudhakkrat,* 74, 81.

339. *Muslimbruder.* See, in particular, the highly insightful section on associations, 86-96.

340. Muhammad Amarah, *Abu al-A^cla al-Maududi,* (Beirut, 1986), 33-34.

341. Information on Hasan al-Banna's ideas and activities is found in his *Mudhakkarat.* Secondary sources include, Muhammad Shawqi Zaki, *al-Ikhwan al-Muslimun wa-al-Mujtama^c al-Misri* (The Muslim Brotherhood and Egyptian Society), (Cairo, 1980 [1952 1st edition]), henceforth *Mujtama^c*; Ishaq Husayni, *al-Ikhwan al-Muslimun: Kubra al-Harakat al-Islamiyyah al-Hadithah* (The Muslim Brotherhood: The Largest Modern Islamic Movement), (Beirut, 1952), henceforth *Kubra*; and Richard P. Mitchell, *The Society of the Muslim Brotherhood,* (Oxford, 1969), henceforth *Society of Brotherhood.*

342. *Mudhakkarat,* 22-23, 24.

343. *Ibid,* 21.

344. *Ibid.*

345. *Ibid,* 24.

346. On examples of this attitude, see W. F. Smalley, "Arabic Newspapers and Mission Work in Syria" in *The Moslem World* (October, 1931), 410.

347. *Mudhakkarat,* 24. See also, *ibid,* 151-152.

348. *Ibid,* 24.

349. *Ibid.*

350. See, for example, *Modern Trends in Islam,* 63.

351. *Mudhakkarat,* 36, 55, respectively.

352. *Ibid,* 254.

353. *Ibid.*

354. *Ibid.*

355. *Ibid,* 74.

356. *Ibid.*

357. *Ibid,* 115-116.

358. *Ibid.,* 76. A concise account of *Ikhwan* is found in: G. Delanoue, "al-Ikwan al-Muslimun", *EI2,* III, 1068-1071.

359. Though this is not explicitly articulated by al-Banna, its implied by some of his writings and affirmed by some important members of *Ikhwan*. See, for example, Mahmud Abd al-Halim, *al-Ikhwan al-Muslimun,* (Alexandria, 1979), 35-35.

360. *Mudhakkarat,* 71.

361. Fred de Jong, "Aspects of the Political Involvement of Sufi Orders in Twentieth Century Egypt (1907-1970)-An Explanatory Stock-Taking" in Gabriel R, Warburg & Uri M. Kupfers Chmidt, eds., *Islam, Nationalism, and Radicalism in Egypt and the Sudan,* (New York, 1983); 199, henceforth *Sufi Orders.*

362. *Ibid.*

363. On the prorogation activity of *Ikhwan* in neighboring villages to al-Ismailiyyah, see *Mudhakkarat,* 87, 99, 101,103-104, 108. On its transfer to Cairo, see *ibid,* 130.

364. Mahmud al-Mutwalli, *Misr wa-al-Hayat al-Hizbiyyah wa-al-Niyabiyyah Qabl Sanat 1952* (Egypt and Political and Parliamentary Life before 1952), (Cairo, 1980), 153-162.

365. Abd al-Rahman al-Rafiᶜi, *Fi Aᶜqab al-Thawrah al-Misriyyah* (In the Aftermath of the Egyptian Revolution), (Cairo, 1951), III, 206-227.

366. Abbas al-Sisi, *Fi Qafilat al-Ikhwan al- Muslimin* (In the Caravan of the Muslim Brotherhood), (Cairo, 1987), I, 140-141, henceforth *Fi Qafilat.*

367. Hasan al-Banna, *Majmuaᶜt Rasa'il al-Imam al-Shahid Hasan al-Banna* (The Collection of The Treatises of al-Imam, the Martyr Hasan al-Banna), (Cairo, 1970?), 272, henceforth *Rasa'il al-Banna.*

368. *Mudhakkarat,* 145.

369. On the sponsorship of benevolent projects by *Ikhwan,* see *Mudhakkarat,* 178-179, 199-200, 249-250. On letters by *Ikhwan* to: King Fuad, see *ibid,* 156-157; to Umar Tusun, *ibid,* 212-213; to Mustafa al-Nahas, *ibid,* 221-222; and to Ali Mahir, *ibid,* 281-266, 268-269. On *Risalat al-Murshid al-ʿAmm,* see *ibid,* 142-143. On *Majallat al-Ikhwan al-Muslimin al-Usbuʿiyyah, ibid,* 143-144. On *Majallat al-Nadhir, ibid,* 144-145. On the anti Christian missionary activity of *Ikhwan,* see *ibid,* 104,140, 151-157.

370. See, for example, *ibid,* 83, 92, 108-110, 216.

371. *Ibid,* 241-243. See also, *Kubra,* 25.

372. Muhammad Shawqi Zaki, *al-Ikhwan al-Muslimun wa-al-Mujtama al-Misri* (The Muslim Brothers and Egyptian Society), (Cairo, 1980 [1952 1st editions]), 26, henceforth *Mujtamaʿ.*

373. *Ibid,* 27.

374. *Fi Qafilat,* I, 92-95.

375. *Mujtamaʿ,* 27.

376. *Ibid,* 28.

377. On the distortion of election results, see *Mujtamaʿ,* 27-28. On the participation of *Ikhwan* in the elections of 1984, see Tariq al-Mahdawi, *al-Ikhwan al-Muslimun ʿala Madhbah al-Munawarah* (The Muslim Brotherhood on the Altar of Political Scheming), (Beirut, 1986), 152-154, henceforth *Munawarah.*

378. *Mudhakkarat,* 258.

379. See, for example, *Rasa'il al-Banna,* 105, 192, 372-376.

380. *Rasa'il al-Banna,* 231; *Mudhakarat,* 258; and *Rasa'il al-Banna,* 248, respectively.

381. *Society of Brotherhood,* 18.

382. *Mudhakkarat,* 267.

383. Abd al-Halim Khafaji, *ʿIndama Ghabat al-Shams* (When the Sun Set), (Kuwait, 1979), 245-254, henceforth *ʿIndama Ghabat.*

384. Fred de Jong, "Turuq and Turuq-Opposition in 20th Century Egypt" in Frithiof Rundgrun, ed., *Proceedings of the VIᵗʰ Congress of Arabic and Islamic Studies* (Leiden, 1972), 90, henceforth *Turuq-Opposition.*

385. *Sufi Orders,* 196-197.

386. *Al-Ahram* (November 18, 1954), 1, 4.

387. On *al-Qumsan al-Khudr*'s link with fascism see Abd al-Azim Muhammad Ramadan, *Tatawwur al-Harakah al-Wataniyyah fi Misr* (The development of the National Movement in Egypt), (Cairo, n.d.), I, 227-234, henceforth *Tatawwur al-Harakah al-Wataniyyah.* On *al-Qumsan al-Zurq*'s link with fascism, see *ibid,* I, 97-108. On *al-Jawwalah*'s link with fascism, see *ibid,* I, 308-315.

388. *Society of Brotherhood*, 314.

389. See Afif Bazri, *al-Jihad fi al-Islam* (Jihad in Islam), (Damascus, 1984); and "Djihad" in *EI2,* 538-540.

390. On the scouting activity of al-Jawwalah, see *Mujtamaᶜ*, 151-154. On the community services of *al-Jawwalah*, see *ibid*, 158-161. On *al-Jawwalah*'s security function, see *Society of Brotherhood,* 202.

391. *Rasa'il al-Banna*, 34.

392. *Fi Qafilat*, I, 233.

393. *Ibid*, I, 60.

394. *Ibid*, I, 203.

395. *Mujtamaᶜ*, 150-152.

396. *Tatawwur al-Harakah al-Wataniyyah*, II, 128.

397. Hasan Dawh, *Safahat Min Jihad al-Shabab al-Muslim* (Pages From the Struggle of the Muslim Youth), (1979?), 26-27; and *Society of Brotherhood,* 60.

398. *Ibid.*

399. *Ibid.*

400. *Mudhakkarat,* 267.

401. *Ibid*, 203.

402. *Ibid*, 211-216.

403. *Society of Brotherhood*, 56.

404. *Mujtamaᶜ,* 32.

405. *Fi Qafilat,* I, 230.

406. *Ibid.*

407. *Ibid*, 57. See also *al-Ahram,* (March 7, 1948), 2, for information on the contributions of *Ikhwan* to the war effort.

408. *Society of Brotherhood*, 78.

409. *Fi Qafilat*, I, 150-151.

410. *Religious and Political Trends*, 99.

411. *Fi Qafilat*, I, 258-259. See also *al-Ahram* (March 23, 1948), 1, for details of the assassination account.

412. *Fi Qafilat*, I, 258.

413. *Ibid*, 259.

414. *Fi Qafilat*, I, 204. See also *al-Ahram* (July 21, 1948), 6; *ibid* (August 2, 1948), 1, 7; and *ibid* (August 4, 1948), 1, 5-6.

415. *Society of Brotherhood*, 75.

416. *Fi Qafilat*, I, 269-275. Sources are unclear on whether or not al-Sandi was among those arrested.

417. *Ibid*, I, 281-283. See also *al-Ahram,* (December 9, 1948), 1-2, for the official announcement.

418. *Fi Qtfilat*, I, 281.

419. *Ibid*, I, 289-299.

420. *Ibid*, I, 283-284.

421. *Kubra,* 35.

422. *Fi Qafilat,* I, 286. See also *al-Ahram,* (December 29, 1948), 1, for details of the assassination account.

423. *Fi Qafilat,* I, 298-299.

424. *Society of Brotherhood*, 68.

425. *Kubra,* 36.

426. al-Banna's letter is reprinted in Jamal Salim, *al-Bulis al-Siyasi Yahkum Misr,* 1910-1952 (The Security Officers Rule Egypt, 1910-1952), (Cairo, n.d.), 326.

427. See *al-Ahram* (February 13,1949), for the assassination account. See *ibid*, (January 9, 1953), 9, for the specification of the charges and the verdicts against al-Banna's assassins.

428. See *al-Ahram,* (December 5,1954), 1, 11, for the specification of the charges and verdicts against *Ikhwan.*

429. See Qutb's statements to his investigators upon his arrest, found in Sami al-Jawhar, *al-Mawta Yatakalamun* (The Dead Speak), (Cairo, 1977), 111-146. See also *al-Ahram,* (August 22,1966), 1, 9, for the specification of the charges and the verdicts against *Ikhwan.*

430. The distinction between expressive and instrumental institutions was introduced by Gordon and Babchuck. See Gordon, Wayne, and Nicholas Babchuk (1959) "Typology of Voluntary Association," in *American Sociological Review*, 24, 22-29.

431. On the nature and impact of depersonalization in the modern world, see, for example, Max Weber, *Economy and Society*, ed. Guenther Roth and Claus Witich (Berkeley, 1978), Vol 2, 637; and Nelson, Benjamin, *The Idea of Usury: From Tribal Brotherhood to Universal Otherhood* (Chicago, 1969).

432. *Fi Qafilat*, I, 150-165.

433. See Nikkie Keddie's essay "Religion and Society in Iran" in her *Iran: Religion, Politics and Society,* (London, 1980); and Dilip Hiro, *Holy Wars,* (New York, 1989). A comparative study of *Sunni* and *Shi^ci* Islamic militancy is found in Ahmad Rif^cat Sayyid, *al-Harakat al-Islamiyyah fi Misr wa-Iran* (The Islamic Movements in Egypt and Iran), (Cairo, 1989).

434. *Tarikh ^cAbduh,* 58-59. See also Edward G. Browne, *The Persian Revolution of 1905-1909,* (London, 1966), 31-58.

435. Zafir al-Qasimi, *Nizam al-Hukm fi al-Shariʿah wa-al-Tarikh al-Islami* (The Political System in Islamic Law and Islamic History), (Beirut, 1974), 244-246.

436. *Aʿmal ʿAbduh*, I, 351.

437. *Manar,* XXVI, 101. Note: emphasis is Rida's.

438. *Rasa'il al-Banna,* 244.

439. One of the few exceptions is Jawdat Said, an important Syrian religious scholar who is a firm believer in nonviolence. See Jawdat Said, *Mafhum al-Taghyir* (Conceptualizing Change), (Damascus, 2001).

440. *Aʿmal ʿAbduh,* I, 727.

Bibliography

The bulk of this book is based on works which contain the writings of al-Afghani, Abduh, Rida and al-Banna and/or which contain primary material regarding their activities, those involving an institutional nature in particular.

I. Primary Sources in the Arabic Language

Afshar, Iraj and Mahdavi, Asghar, eds., *Majmu̇ʿyi Asnad va Madarik-i Jap Nishuda Darbara-yi Jamal al-Din Mashhur bi Afghani* (A Collection of Previously Unpublished Documents and Notes Concerning Jamal al-Din, better known as al-Afghani) (Tehran, 1963).

Allush , Naji, ed., *Adib Ishaq, al-Kitabat al-Siyasiyyah wa-al-Ijtimaʿiyyah* (Adib Ishaq, The Political and Social Works), (Beirut, 1978).

Amarah, Muhammad, ed., *Jamal al-Din al-Afghani: al-Aʿmal al-Siyasiyyah* (Jamal al-Din al-Afghani: The Political Works), (Beirut, 1979).

Amarah, Muhammad, ed., *al-Aʿmal al-Kamilah Li-al-lmam Muhammad ʿAbduh* (The Complete Works of Muhammad ʿAbduh), (Beirut, 1972).

Arslan, Shakib, *al-Amir Shakib Arslan, Sirah Dhatiyyah* (The Prince Shakib Arslan, A Personal Memoir), (Beirut, 1969).

Arslan, Shakib, *al-Sayyid Rashid Rida, aw Ikha' Arbaʿin ʿam* (al-Sayyid Rashid Rida Or Fourty Years of Friendship), (Damascus, 1937).

al-Banna, Hasan, *Mudhakkarat al-Daʿwah wa-al-Daʿiyyah* (Memoirs of the Message and of the Messenger), (Cairo, 1978).

al-Banna, Hasan, *Majmuʿat Rasa'il al-lmam al-Shahid Hasan al-Banna* (The Collection of The Treatises of al-lmam, the Martyr Hasan al-Banna), (Cairo, 1970?).

Darwazah, Muhammad Izzat, *Nash'at al-Harakah al-ʿArabiyyah al-Hadithah* (The Rise of the Modern Arab Movement), (Beirut, 1971).

Ibish, Yusuf, ed., *Rihlat al-Imam Muhammad Rashid Rida,* (Beirut, 1971).

Ibn Ashur, Muhammad al-Fadil, *al-Harakah al-Adabiyyah wa-al-Fikriyyah Fi Tunis* (The Literary and Intellectual Movement in Tunis), (Tunis, 1972).

Ishaq, Awni, ed., *al-Durar* (The Pearls), (Beirut, 1909).

al-Jabarti, Abd al-Rahman, *ᶜAja'ib al-Athar fi al-Tarajim wa-al-Akhbar* (The Marvelous Events that Occurred in Biographies and Accounts), (Cairo, 1958).

al-Jabarti, ᶜAbd al-Rahman, *Mazhar al-Taqdis bi-Dhihab Dawlat al-Firansis,*(The Reveleation of Glory Through the Termination of the French Occupation), Jawharah, Hasan M. & Disuqi, Umar, eds., (Cairo, 1969).

"al-Jamᶜiyyat fi al-Islam" in *al-Hilal,* XXXVI, (April, 1, 1918).

Jaridat al-ᶜUrwah al-Wuthqah (Journal of The Firm Bond), Dar al-Arab, ed., (Cairo, 1957).

al-Jawhar, Sami, *al-Mawta Yatakalamun* (The Dead Speak), (Cairo, 1977).

Khafaji, Abd al-Halim, *ᶜIndama Ghabat al-Shams* (When the Sun Set), (Kuwait, 1979).

Kurd Ali, Muhammad, *al-Muᶜasirun* (The Contemporaries), al-Misri, Muhammad, ed., (Damscus, 1980).

al-Makhzumi, Muhammad, *Khatirat Jamal al-Din al-Afghani* (The Reflections of Jamal al-Din al-Afghani), (Beirut, 1931).

al-Munajid, Salah al-Din & Khuri, Yusuf Q., eds., *Fatawa al-Imam Muhammad Rashid Rida* (The Religious Legal Verdicts of Muhammad Rashid Rida), (Beirut, 1970).

Rida, Rashid, *Tafsir al-Manar* (The Qur'anic Exegeses of Manar), (Cairo, 1954).

Rida, Rashid, *Tarikh al-Ustadh al-Imam Muhammad ᶜAbduh* (Biography of the Teacher, the Imam, Muhammad 'Abduh), Vols. I-III, (Cairo, 1931).

Rida, Rashid, ed., *Majallat al-Manar* (The Journal of the Beacon), Vols. I-XXXIV, (1898-1935).

Rida, Rashid, *al-Manar wa-al-Azhar* (Al-Manar and al-Azhar), (Cairo, 1935).

Said, Amin, *Asrar al-Thawrah al-ᶜArabiyyah al-Kubra* (Secrets of the Great Arab Revolt), (Cairo, n.d.).

Said, Amin, *al-Thawrah al-ᶜArabiyyah al-Kubra* (The Great Arab Revolt), (Cairo, n.d.).

Salim, Jamal, *al-Bulis al-Siyasi Yahkum Misr, 1910-1952* (The Security Officers Rule Egypt), (Cairo, n.d.).

Sannu Yacqub, ed., *Suhuf Abu Nazzarah Zarka', 1878-1900,* (The Journals of Abu Nazzarah Zarqa', 1878-1900), (Beirut, n.d.).

Shalsh, Ali, ed., *Jamal al-Din al-Afghani: al-ᶜAmal al-Majhulah* (Jamal al-Din al-Afghani: The Unknown Works), (London, 1987).

Shalsh, Ali, *Muhammad ᶜAbduh, al-Aᶜmal al-Majhulah* (Muhammad -Abduh, The Unknown Works), (London, 1987).

al-Sisi, Abbas, *Fi Qafilat al-Ikhwan al-Muslimun* (In the Caravan of the Muslim Brothers), (Cairo, 1987).

al-Talibi, Ammar, *Ibn Badis, Hayatuhu wa-Atharuhu* (Ibn Badis, His Life and Works), I-IV, (Algiers, 1968).

Tarrazi, Filib di, *Tarikh al-Sahafah al-ᶜArabiyah* (History of Arab Journalism), (Beirut, 1913).

al-Turk, Niqula, *Dhikr Tamaluk Jumhur al-Faransawiyyah bi-al-Aqtar al-Misriyyah wa-al-Bilad al-Shamiyyah* (The Account of the French Campaign on Egypt and Syria), (Beirut, 1990 [first published in 1839]).

Zaydan, Jurji, *Tarikh al-Masuniyah al-ᶜAm* (History of Freemasonry), (Cairo, 1889).

Zaydan, Jurji, *Tarikh Adab al-Lughah al-ᶜArabiyyah,* (History of Arabic Literature), Vol. I-IV, (Cairo, 1957).

Zaydan, Jurji, *Majllat al-Hilal,* (Cairo, 1892-Still Published).

II. Primary Sources in European Languages

Blunt, Wilfrid Scawen, *Secret History of the English Occupation of Egypt,* (New York: A. A. Knopf, 1922).

Broadly, A. M., *How We Defended Arabi and His Friends: A Story of Egypt and the Egyptians* (London: Chapman & Hall Ltd., 1884).

Gould, Robert Freke, *The History of Freemasonry,* (London: John C. Yorston & Co., 1887).

Lavauzelle, H. Charles , ed., C. La Jonquiere, *L'Expedition francaise en Egypte* (1798-1801), I-V, (Paris: J. M. Eberhart, 1899-1907).

Kampffmayer, G., "Egypt and Western Asia" in H.A.R. Gibb, ed., *Whither Islam?*, (London: AMS Press, 1932).

Sabry, Mohammed, *La genese de l'esprit national egyptien (1863-82)* (The Genesis of the National Egyptian Spirit), (Paris: Association Cinotypiste, 1924).

www.ingramcontent.com/pod-product-compliance
Lightning Source LLC
Chambersburg PA
CBHW031602110426
42742CB00036B/679